Name _____ Class _____ 1

Skills Worksheet

Concept Review

Section: Oxidation-Reduction Reactions

Choose the statement from Column B that best matches the term in Column A, and write the corresponding letter in the space provided.

Column A

_____ **1.** reduction

_____ **2.** oxidation

_____ **3.** redox reaction

_____ **4.** oxidation number

_____ **5.** reducing agent

_____ **6.** half-reaction

_____ **7.** oxidizing agent

Column B

a. a chemical reaction in which a substance gains electrons

b. any chemical process in which electrons are transferred from one substance to another

c. a chemical reaction in which a substance loses electrons

d. substance that causes reduction to happen and is itself oxidized

e. number assigned to an atom in a poly-atomic ion or molecular compound based on the assumption of complete transfer of electrons

f. substance that causes the oxidation of other substances and is itself reduced

g. the part of a reaction that involves only oxidation or reduction

Determine the oxidation number for each atom in the following chemical formulas.

8. $ZnCl_2$

9. SO_3

10. HNO_3

11. $Al_2(SO_4)_3$

12. PbO

W1

13. CO_2

14. H_2SO_4

15. Write the half-reaction for the conversion of hydrogen peroxide to water.

16. Identify which of the following reactions is a reduction reaction and which is an oxidation reaction. Write the balanced overall ionic equation for the redox reaction between these two.

$$Mg \rightarrow Mg^{2+} + 2e^-$$

$$O_2 + 4e^- \rightarrow 2O^{2-}$$

Balance the following equations using the half-reaction method.

17. $MnO_2^- + SO_2 \rightarrow SO_4^{2-} + Mn^{2+}$ (in acidic solution)

18. $NO_3^- + Cu \rightarrow NO + Cu^{2+}$ (in acidic solution)

19. $H_2S + NO_3^- \rightarrow NO_2 + S_8$ (in acidic solution)

20. In this equation identify which atoms where reduced and which were oxidized.

$$2K(s) + Cl_2(g) \rightarrow 2KCl(s)$$

_____

_____

Skills Worksheet

Concept Review

Section: Introduction to Electrochemistry

Complete the following statements by choosing a term from the following list. Use each term only once.

electric current   voltage   electrochemical cell   electrode   amperes

1. The _____ of a cell is a measure of its ability to do electrical work.

2. The movement of electrons or other charged particles is described as

_____, and is expressed in units of _____.

3. A(n) _____ is a conductor that connects with a nonmetallic part of a circuit.

4. A(n) _____ consists of two electrodes separated by an electrolyte.

Choose the statement from Column B that best matches the term in Column A, and write the corresponding letter in the space provided.

Column A

_____ **5.** electrolytes

_____ **6.** metals

_____ **7.** electrode

_____ **8.** cathode

_____ **9.** electrode reactions

_____**10.** anode

_____**11.** cathodic reaction

_____**12.** anodic reaction

Column B

a. the electrode at which oxidation takes place

b. conductors in which electrons carry charges

c. conductors in which ions in solution carry charges

d. the electrode at which reduction takes place

e. a conductor in electrical contact with an electrolyte solution

f. reactions that involve the transfer of electrons at the electrodes of a cell

g. a reaction in which electrons are released at the anode

h. a reaction in which electrons are consumed at the cathode

| Concept Review continued

Complete each statement below by writing the correct term or phrase.

13. An anode must be paired with a _____ for a redox reaction to occur.

14. The simplest electrochemical cell consists of two pieces of metal in an

_____ solution.

15. The anode is wherever _____ is going on.

16. A cathode is wherever _____ is going on.

17. In an electrochemical cell, a _____ keeps electrolyte solutions from mixing, but lets ions move.

Solve the following problems, and write your answers in the space provided.

18. Explain how electrons move between the negative and positive terminals in a typical flashlight battery.

_____

_____

_____

19. Write an electrode reaction in which you change $Zn(s)$ to $Zn^{+2}(aq)$. Would this reaction happen at an anode or a cathode?

20. Write an electrode reaction which would occur at a cathode and which involves Cu^{2+}. Is this reaction oxidation or reduction?

Skills Worksheet)

Concept Review

Section: Galvanic Cells

Complete each statement by underlining the correct word in brackets.

1. In concept, fuel cells are very [simple, complex].

2. The fuel cell in your text shows that the fuel and oxidizer are supplied to [two, four] electrodes from [outside, within] the cell. The [two, four] electrodes are separated by a [thick, thin] layer of electrolyte.

3. In conventional power plants, chemical energy in fuel is [directly, indirectly] turned into electrical energy; the process is [efficient, inefficient].

4. The fuel cell [directly, indirectly] converts chemical energy into electrical energy; the process is [simple, difficult] and [efficient, inefficient].

5. Perfectly efficient energy conversion is theoretically [possible, impossible] with fuel cells.

6. Batteries are self-contained [galvanic, electrolytic] cells.

7. Batteries convert [electrical, chemical] energy into [electrical, chemical] energy.

8. The battery is a [fixed, portable] means of energy.

9. The common zinc-carbon battery is a(n) [acidic, alkaline] cell.

10. The [alkaline, lead-acid] cell is a newer, better version of the acidic cell.

11. Dry cells are not dry; a [carbon, zinc] rod, the battery's positive terminal, contacts a wet paste.

12. The batteries in electronic devices around your home are probably [acidic, alkaline] cells.

13. A [steel, paper] outer shell is needed to prevent caustic contents from leaking out of an alkaline cell.

14. The standard automobile battery is a [lead-, zinc-] acid storage cell.

15. [Lead(II) sulfate, copper(II) sulfate] is produced at both electrodes in an automobile battery.

16. When an automobile battery discharges, it acts as a [galvanic, electrolytic] cell; when it recharges, it functions as an [galvanic, electrolytic] cell.

17. The energy to drive the [recharging, discharging] of an automobile battery comes from an internal source, such as the car's engine.

18. [Galvanic, Electrolytic] cells generate electrical energy.

19. A [Daniell, Downs] cell converts chemical energy into electrical energy.

❙ Concept Review *continued*

Solve the following problems, and write your answers in the space provided.

20. Calculate the voltage of a cell for the reaction between a silver electrode in a solution containing silver ions and a zinc electrode in a solution containing zinc ions. Identify the anode and the cathode.

21. Calculate the voltage of a cell for the reaction between a copper electrode in a solution containing copper(II) ions and a lead electrode in a solution containing lead(II) ions. Identify the anode and the cathode.

22. Write the electrochemical equation for the reaction that will naturally occur in a cell that contains a zinc, Zn^{2+}/Zn, electrode and a copper, Cu^{2+}/Cu, electrode.

23. Write the electrochemical equation for the reaction that will naturally occur in a cell that contains a chlorine, Cl_2, electrode and an iodine, I_2, electrode.

24. Write the electrochemical equation for the reaction that will naturally occur in a cell that contains a silver, Ag^+/Ag, electrode and a copper, Cu^{2+}/Cu, electrode.

Answer the following items in the space provided.

25. Define *corrosion*.

_____

_____

_____

26. List the three ingredients generally required in the corrosion of metals.

_____

_____

_____

27. Explain why corrosion is more likely to occur when two different metals are in contact with one another. Give an example.

_____

_____

_____

_____

28. Describe cathodic protection.

_____

_____

_____

_____

_____

_____

Name _____ Class _____ Date _____

Concept Review

Section: Electrolytic Cells

For questions 1–8, complete each statement below by referring to Figure 1 and choosing a term from the following list. Use each term only once.

Figure 1

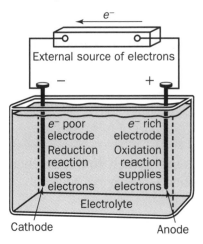

cathode	electrolysis	negative	released	Downs cell	reduction
anode	electrosynthesis	electrolytic	positive	Downs	
nonspontaneous	electrical	oxidation	consumed	molten	

1. _____ cells are electrochemical cells in which _____ chemical reactions are made to occur by an external source of _____ energy.

2. Sodium is manufactured by the _____ of _____ sodium chloride. This method is named the _____ process and is carried out industrially in an electrolytic cell, the _____.

3. Electrons are _____ at the anode (_____) and _____ at the cathode (_____); therefore, electrons travel through the wire from _____ to _____.

4. Since the reaction is nonspontaneous, the external power source forces electrons to flow from the _____ electrode (anode) to the _____ electrode (cathode), as in all electrolytic cells.

5. The _____ of sodium uses electrical energy.

Concept Review *continued*

Answer the following items in the space provided.

6. The equation for the cathodic reaction is _____.

7. The equation for the anodic reaction is _____.

8. The equation for the net reaction is _____.

Complete each statement below by writing the correct term or phrase.

9. _____ occurs at the cathode during the electrolysis of water.

10. The _____ is the positive electrode in the electrolysis of water.

11. In the electrolysis of water, _____ is produced at the anode and

_____ at the cathode.

12. An _____ is added to water to make it an effective conductor
during electrolysis, but the electrolyte does not undergo any redox reactions.

13. Electrolytic cells are used to _____ metals.

14. Electrolytic cells convert _____ energy into _____
energy by using an external power source.

**Choose the statement from Column B that best matches the term in Column A, and
write the corresponding letter in the space provided.**

Column A

_____**15.** bauxite

_____**16.** Hall-Héroult

_____**17.** 5%

_____**18.** molten cryolite

_____**19.** carbon-lined
tank

_____**20.** carbon rods

_____**21.** 95%

_____**22.** electroplating

Column B

a. function as anodes in the Hall-Héroult process

b. name given to the electrochemical process of
obtaining aluminum from its ore

c. serves as the cathode in the Hall-Héroult process

d. ore of aluminum

e. an electrochemical process in which a metal ion
is reduced and a solid metal is deposited on a
surface

f. percentage of electrical energy consumed in
the United States to produce aluminum

g. the percentage of the cost that can be saved by
recycling aluminum cans as opposed to
producing aluminum cans from bauxite ore

h. Na_3AlF_6; used to dissolve alumina at 970°C

Problem Solving

Redox Equations

The feature that distinguishes redox reactions from other types of reactions is that elements change oxidation state by gaining or losing electrons. Compare the equations for the following two reactions:

$$(1)\ \text{KBr}(aq) + \text{AgNO}_3(aq) \rightarrow \text{AgBr}(s) + \text{KNO}_3(aq)$$

$$(2)\ 2\text{KBr}(aq) + \text{Cl}_2(g) \rightarrow 2\text{KCl}(aq) + \text{Br}_2(l)$$

Equation 1 represents the combining of the salts potassium bromide solution and a silver nitrate solution to form a precipitate of insoluble silver bromide, leaving potassium nitrate in solution. The only change that occurs is that ions trade places, forming an insoluble compound. This reaction is a typical double-replacement reaction. It is driven by the removal of Ag^+ and Br^- from solution in the form of a precipitate.

You will recognize that Equation 2 is a single-replacement reaction in which chlorine atoms replace bromine atoms in the salt KBr. Although it is not complex, Equation 2 differs from Equation 1 in a fundamental way. In order for chlorine to replace bromine, the uncharged atoms of elemental chlorine must change into chloride ions, each having a $1-$ charge. Also, bromide ions with a $1-$ charge must change into uncharged bromine atoms. The K^+ is a spectator ion that doesn't participate in the process. In fact, it could be Na^+, Ca^{2+}, Fe^{3+}, H^+, or any other stable cation.

The loss of electrons by bromine is oxidation, and the gain of electrons by chlorine is reduction.

Formation of the chloride ions and the bromine molecule involves the complete transfer of two electrons. The two chlorine atoms gain two electrons, and two bromide ions lose two electrons. Oxidation and reduction can involve the partial transfer of electrons as well as the complete transfer seen in the preceding example. The oxidation number of an atom is not synonymous with the charge on that atom, so a change in oxidation number does not require a change in actual charge. Take the example of the following half-reaction:

$$\text{H}_2\text{C}_2\text{O}_4(aq) \rightarrow 2\text{CO}_2(g) + 2\text{H}^+(aq) + 2e^-$$

Carbon changes oxidation state from $+3$ to $+4$. Carbon is oxidized even though it is not ionized.

The potassium bromide–chlorine reaction is simple, but many redox reactions are not. In this worksheet, you will practice the art of balancing redox equations and try your hand at more-complex ones.

Problem Solving *continued*

There are seven simple steps to balancing redox equations. You will find these steps in the General Plan for Balancing Redox Equations.

General Plan for Balancing Redox Equations

1 Write the unbalanced formula equation if it is not given. List formulas for any ionic substances as their individual ions, and write a total ionic equation.

2 Assign oxidation numbers to each element. Then rewrite the equation, leaving out any ions or molecules whose elements do not change oxidation state during the reaction.

3 Write the half-reaction for reduction. You must decide which element of the ions and molecules left after item 2 is reduced. Once you have written the half-reaction, you must balance it for charge and mass.

4 Write the half-reaction for oxidation. You must decide which element of the ions and molecules left after item 2 is oxidized. Once you have written the half-reaction, you must balance it for charge and mass.

5 Adjust the coefficients of the two half-reactions so that the same number of electrons are gained in reduction as are lost in oxidation.

6 Add the two half-reactions together. Cancel out anything common to both sides of the new equation. Note that the electrons should always cancel out of the total equation.

7 Combine ions to form the compounds shown in the original formula equation. Check to ensure that all other ions and atoms balance.

| Problem Solving *continued*

REACTIONS IN ACIDIC SOLUTION

Sample Problem 1

Write a balanced redox equation for the reaction of hydrochloric acid with nitric acid to produce aqueous hypochlorous acid and nitrogen monoxide.

Solution

ANALYZE

What is given in the problem? the reactants and products of a redox reaction

What are you asked to find? the balanced redox reaction

Items	Data
Reactants	HCl, HNO_3
Products	$HClO$, NO
Solution type	acidic
Oxidized species	?
Reduced species	?
Balanced equation	?

PLAN

What steps are needed to balance the redox equation?

1. Write the unbalanced formula equation followed by the ionic equation.
2. Assign oxidation numbers to each element. Delete any ion or molecule in which there is no change in oxidation state.
3. Write the half-reaction for reduction, and balance the mass and charge. H^+ and H_2O may be added to either side of the equation to balance mass.
4. Repeat step 3 for the oxidation half-reaction.
5. Adjust the coefficients so that the number of electrons lost equals the number of electrons gained.
6. Combine the half-reactions, and cancel anything common to both sides of the equation.
7. Combine ions to change the equation back to its original form, and check the balance of everything.

COMPUTE

1. Write the formula equation.

$$HCl(aq) + HNO_3(aq) \rightarrow HClO(aq) + NO(g)$$

Write the total ionic equation.

$$H^+ + Cl^- + H^+ + NO_3^- \rightarrow H^+ + ClO^- + NO$$

Problem Solving *continued*

2. Assign oxidation numbers to each element.

$$\overset{+1}{H^+} + \overset{-1}{Cl^-} + \overset{+1}{H^+} + \overset{+5-2}{NO_3^-} \rightarrow \overset{+1}{H^+} + \overset{-2+1}{OCl^-} + \overset{+2-2}{NO}$$

Delete any ion or molecule in which there is no change in oxidation state.

$$\overset{-1}{Cl^-} + \overset{+5}{NO_3^-} \rightarrow \overset{+1}{OCl^-} + \overset{+2}{NO}$$

3. Write the half-reaction for reduction.

$$\overset{+5}{NO_3^-} \rightarrow \overset{+2}{NO}$$

Balance the mass by adding H^+ and H_2O.

$$4H^+ + \overset{+5}{NO_3^-} \rightarrow \overset{+2}{NO} + 2H_2O$$

Balance the charge by adding electrons to the side with the higher positive charge.

$$4H^+ + \overset{+5}{NO_3^-} + 3e^- \rightarrow \overset{+2}{NO} + 2H_2O$$

4. Write the half-reaction for oxidation.

$$\overset{-1}{Cl^-} \rightarrow \overset{+1}{OCl^-}$$

Balance the mass by adding H^+ and H_2O.

$$\overset{-1}{Cl^-} + H_2O \rightarrow \overset{+1}{OCl^-} + 2H^+$$

Balance charge by adding electrons to the side with the higher positive charge.

$$\overset{-1}{Cl^-} + H_2O \rightarrow \overset{+1}{OCl^-} + 2H^+ + 2e^-$$

5. Multiply by factors so that the number of electrons lost equals the number of electrons gained.

$2e^-$ are lost in oxidation; $3e^-$ are gained in reduction. Therefore, to get $6e^-$ on both sides, calculate as follows:

$$2 \times [4H^+ + NO_3^- + 3e^- \rightarrow NO + 2H_2O]$$
$$3 \times [Cl^- + H_2O \rightarrow OCl^- + 2H^+ + 2e^-]$$

6. Combine the half-reactions.

$$2 \times [4H^+ + NO_3^- + 3e^- \rightarrow NO + 2H_2O]$$
$$+ 3 \times [Cl^- + H_2O \rightarrow OCl^- + 2H^+ + e^-]$$

$$\overline{3Cl^- + 3H_2O + 2NO_3^- + 8H^+ + 6e^- \rightarrow 3OCl^- + 6H^+ + 6e^- + 2NO + 4H_2O}$$

Cancel out anything common to both sides of the equation.

$$3Cl^- + 3\cancel{H_2O}^{2} + 2NO_3^- + \cancel{8}H^+ + \cancel{6e^-} \rightarrow 3OCl^- + \cancel{6}H^+ + \cancel{6e^-} + 2NO + \cancel{4}H_2O$$

7. Combine ions to change the equation back to its original form. There must be five H^+ ions on the reactant side of the equation to bind with the three chloride ions and two nitrate ions, so three H^+ ions must be added to each side.

$$3Cl^- + 2NO_3^- + 5H^+ \rightarrow 3OCl^- + 2NO + H_2O + 3H^+$$

$$3HCl + 2HNO_3 \rightarrow 3HOCl + 2NO + H_2O$$

Check the balance.

| Problem Solving *continued*

EVALUATE

Are the units correct?

NA

Is the number of significant figures correct?

NA

Is the answer reasonable?

Yes; the reaction has the reactants and products required and is balanced.

Practice

Balance the following redox equations. Assume that all reactions take place in an acid environment where H$^+$ and H$_2$O are readily available.

1. $Fe + SnCl_4 \rightarrow FeCl_3 + SnCl_2$ **ans: $2Fe + 3SnCl_4 \rightarrow 2FeCl_3 + 3SnCl_2$**

2. $H_2O_2 + FeSO_4 + H_2SO_4 \rightarrow Fe_2(SO_4)_3 + H_2O$ **ans: $H_2O_2 + 2FeSO_4 + H_2SO_4 \rightarrow Fe_2(SO_4)_3 + 2H_2O$**

3. $CuS + HNO_3 \rightarrow Cu(NO_3)_2 + NO + S + H_2O$ **ans: $3CuS + 8HNO_3 \rightarrow 3Cu(NO_3)_2 + 2NO + 3S + 4H_2O$**

4. $K_2Cr_2O_7 + HI \rightarrow CrI_3 + KI + I_2 + H_2O$ **ans: $K_2Cr_2O_7 + 14HI \rightarrow 2CrI_3 + 2KI + 3I_2 + 7H_2O$**

| Problem Solving *continued*

REACTIONS IN BASIC SOLUTION

Sample Problem 2

Write a balanced equation for the reaction in a basic solution of NiO_2 and Fe to produce $Ni(OH)_2$ and $Fe(OH)_2$.

Solution

ANALYZE

What is given in the problem?　　the reactants and products of a redox reaction

What are you asked to find?　　the balanced redox reaction

Items	Data
Reactants	NiO_2, Fe
Products	$Ni(OH)_2$, $Fe(OH)_2$
Solution type	basic
Oxidized species	?
Reduced species	?
Balanced equation	?

PLAN

What steps are needed to balance the redox equation?

1. Write the formula equation followed by the ionic equation.
2. Assign oxidation numbers to each element. Delete any ion or molecule in which there is no change in oxidation state.
3. Write the half-reaction for reduction, and balance the mass and charge. OH^- and H_2O may be added to either side.
4. Repeat step 3 for the oxidation half-reaction.
5. Adjust the coefficients so that the number of electrons lost equals the number of electrons gained.
6. Combine the half-reactions, and cancel anything common to both sides of the equation.
7. Combine ions to change the equation back to its original form, and check the balance of everything.

COMPUTE

1. Write the formula equation.

$$NiO_2 + Fe \rightarrow Ni(OH)_2 + Fe(OH)_2$$

Write the total ionic equation.

$$NiO_2 + Fe \rightarrow Ni^{2+} + 2OH^- + Fe^{2+} + 2OH^-$$

| Problem Solving *continued*

2. Assign oxidation numbers to each element.

$$\overset{+4-2}{NiO_2} + \overset{0}{Fe} \rightarrow \overset{+2}{Ni^{2+}} + \overset{-2+1}{2OH^-} + \overset{+2}{Fe^{2+}} + \overset{-2+1}{2OH^-}$$

Delete any ions or molecules in which there is no change in oxidation state.

$$\overset{+4}{NiO_2} + \overset{0}{Fe} \rightarrow \overset{+2}{Ni^{2+}} + \overset{+2}{Fe^{2+}}$$

3. Write the half-reaction for reduction.

$$\overset{+4}{NiO_2} \rightarrow \overset{+2}{Ni^{2+}}$$

Balance the mass by adding OH^- and H_2O.

$$\overset{+4}{NiO_2} + 2H_2O \rightarrow \overset{+2}{Ni^{2+}} + 4OH^-$$

Balance the charge by adding electrons to the side with the higher positive charge.

$$\overset{+4}{NiO_2} + 2H_2O + 2e^- \rightarrow \overset{+2}{Ni^{2+}} + 4OH^-$$

4. Write the half-reaction for oxidation.

$$\overset{0}{Fe} \rightarrow \overset{+2}{Fe^{2+}}$$

The mass is already balanced.
Balance the charge by adding electrons to the side with the higher positive charge.

$$\overset{0}{Fe} \rightarrow \overset{+2}{Fe^{2+}} + 2e^-$$

5. The numbers of electrons lost and gained are already the same.

6. Combine the half-reactions.

$$\overset{+4}{NiO_2} + 2H_2O + 2e^- \rightarrow \overset{+2}{Ni^{2+}} + 4OH^-$$
$$+ \overset{0}{Fe} \rightarrow \overset{+2}{Fe^{2+}} + 2e^-$$
$$\overline{NiO_2 + 2H_2O + Fe \rightarrow Ni^{2+} + Fe^{2+} + 4OH^-}$$

7. Combine ions to change the equation back to its original form. The four OH^- ions combine with the nickel and iron to make nickel(II) hydroxide and iron(II) hydroxide.

$$NiO_2 + 2H_2O + Fe \rightarrow Ni(OH)_2 + Fe(OH)_2$$

Check the balance.

EVALUATE
Are the units correct?
NA

Is the number of significant figures correct?
NA

Is the answer reasonable?
Yes; the reaction has the reactants and products required and is balanced.

| **Problem Solving** *continued*

Practice

Balance the following redox equations. Assume that all reactions take place in a basic environment where OH⁻ and H₂O are readily available.

1. $CO_2 + NH_2OH \rightarrow CO + N_2 + H_2O$ **ans: $CO_2 + 2NH_2OH \rightarrow CO + N_2 + 3H_2O$**

2. $Bi(OH)_3 + K_2SnO_2 \rightarrow Bi + K_2SnO_3$ (Both of the potassium-tin-oxygen compounds dissociate into potassium ions and tin-oxygen ions.)
ans: $2Bi(OH)_3 + 3K_2SnO_2 \rightarrow 2Bi + 3K_2SnO_3 + 3H_2O$

Additional Problems

Balance each of the following redox equations. Unless stated otherwise, assume that the reaction occurs in acidic solution.

1. $Mg + N_2 \rightarrow Mg_3N_2$

2. $SO_2 + Br_2 + H_2O \rightarrow HBr + H_2SO_4$

3. $H_2S + Cl_2 \rightarrow S + HCl$

4. $PbO_2 + HBr \rightarrow PbBr_2 + Br_2 + H_2O$

5. $S + HNO_3 \rightarrow NO_2 + H_2SO_4 + H_2O$

6. $NaIO_3 + N_2H_4 + HCl \rightarrow N_2 + NaICl_2 + H_2O$ (N_2H_4 is hydrazine; do not separate it into ions.)

7. $MnO_2 + H_2O_2 + HCl \rightarrow MnCl_2 + O_2 + H_2O$

8. $AsH_3 + NaClO_3 \rightarrow H_3AsO_4 + NaCl$ (AsH_3 is arsine, the arsenic analogue of ammonia, NH_3.)

9. $K_2Cr_2O_7 + H_2C_2O_4 + HCl \rightarrow CrCl_3 + CO_2 + KCl + H_2O$ ($H_2C_2O_4$ is oxalic acid; it can be treated as $2H^+ + C_2O_4^{2-}$.)

10. $Hg(NO_3)_2 \xrightarrow{\text{heat}} HgO + NO_2 + O_2$ (The reaction is not in solution.)

11. $HAuCl_4 + N_2H_4 \rightarrow Au + N_2 + HCl$ ($HAuCl_4$ can be considered as $H^+ + AuCl_4^-$.)

12. $Sb_2(SO_4)_3 + KMnO_4 + H_2O \rightarrow H_3SbO_4 + K_2SO_4 + MnSO_4 + H_2SO_4$

13. $Mn(NO_3)_2 + NaBiO_3 + HNO_3 \rightarrow Bi(NO_3)_2 + HMnO_4 + NaNO_3 + H_2O$

14. $H_3AsO_4 + Zn + HCl \rightarrow AsH_3 + ZnCl_2 + H_2O$

15. $KClO_3 + HCl \rightarrow Cl_2 + H_2O + KCl$

16. The same reactants as in Item 15 can combine in the following way when more $KClO_3$ is present. Balance the equation.

$$KClO_3 + HCl \rightarrow Cl_2 + ClO_2 + H_2O + KCl$$

17. $MnCl_3 + H_2O \rightarrow MnCl_2 + MnO_2 + HCl$

18. $NaOH + H_2O + Al \rightarrow NaAl(OH)_4 + H_2$ in basic solution

19. $Br_2 + Ca(OH)_2 \rightarrow CaBr_2 + Ca(BrO_3)_2 + H_2O$ in basic solution

20. $N_2O + NaClO + NaOH \rightarrow NaCl + NaNO_2 + H_2O$ in basic solution

21. Balance the following reaction, which can be used to prepare bromine in the laboratory:

$$HBr + MnO_2 \rightarrow MnBr_2 + H_2O + Br_2$$

22. The following reaction occurs when gold is dissolved in *aqua regia*. Balance the equation.

$$Au + HCl + HNO_3 \rightarrow HAuCl_4 + NO + H_2O$$

Skills Worksheet

Problem Solving

Electrochemistry

The potential in volts has been measured for many different reduction half-reactions. The potential value is measured against the standard hydrogen electrode, which is assigned a value of zero. For consistency, these half-reactions are always written in the direction of the reduction. A half-reaction that has a positive reduction potential proceeds in the direction of the reduction when it is coupled with a hydrogen electrode. A reaction that has a negative reduction potential proceeds in the oxidation direction when it is coupled with a hydrogen electrode. **Table 1** gives some common standard reduction potentials.

TABLE 1

Reduction half-reaction	Standard electrode potential, E^0 (in volts)	Reduction half-reaction	Standard electrode potential, E^0 (in volts)
$MnO_4^- + 8H^+ + 5e^- \rightleftharpoons Mn^{2+} + 4H_2O$	+1.50	$Fe^{3+} + 3e^- \rightleftharpoons Fe$	−0.04
$Au^{3+} + 3e^- \rightleftharpoons Au$	+1.50	$Pb^{2+} + 2e^- \rightleftharpoons Pb$	−0.13
$Cl_2 + 2e^- \rightleftharpoons 2Cl^-$	+1.36	$Sn^{2+} + 2e^- \rightleftharpoons Sn$	−0.14
$Cr_2O_7^{2-} + 14H^+ + 6e^- \rightleftharpoons 2Cr^{3+} + 7H_2O$	+1.23	$Ni^{2+} + 2e^- \rightleftharpoons Ni$	−0.26
$MnO_2 + 4H^+ + 2e^- \rightleftharpoons Mn^{2+} + 2H_2O$	+1.22	$Cd^{2+} + 2e^- \rightleftharpoons Cd$	−0.40
$Br_2 + 2e^- \rightleftharpoons 2Br^-$	+1.07	$Fe^{2+} + 2e^- \rightleftharpoons Fe$	−0.45
$Hg^{2+} + 2e^- \rightleftharpoons Hg$	+0.85	$S + 2e^- \rightleftharpoons S^{2-}$	−0.48
$Ag^+ + e^- \rightleftharpoons Ag$	+0.80	$Zn^{2+} + 2e^- \rightleftharpoons Zn$	−0.76
$Hg_2^{2+} + 2e^- \rightleftharpoons 2Hg$	+0.80	$Al^{3+} + 3e^- \rightleftharpoons Al$	−1.66
$Fe^{3+} + e^- \rightleftharpoons Fe^{2+}$	+0.77	$Mg^{2+} + 2e^- \rightleftharpoons Mg$	−2.37
$MnO_4^- + e^- \rightleftharpoons MnO_4^{2-}$	+0.56	$Na^+ + e^- \rightleftharpoons Na$	−2.71
$I_2 + 2e^- \rightleftharpoons 2I^-$	+0.54	$Ca^{2+} + 2e^- \rightleftharpoons Ca$	−2.87
$Cu^{2+} + 2e^- \rightleftharpoons Cu$	+0.34	$Ba^{2+} + 2e^- \rightleftharpoons Ba$	−2.91
$S + 2H^+(aq) + 2e^- \rightleftharpoons H_2S(aq)$	+0.14	$K^+ + e^- \rightleftharpoons K$	−2.93
$2H^+(aq) + 2e^- \rightleftharpoons H_2$	+0.00	$Li^+ + e^- \rightleftharpoons Li$	−3.04

Problem Solving *continued*

You can use reduction potentials to predict the direction in which any redox reaction will be spontaneous. A spontaneous reaction occurs by itself, without outside influence. The redox reaction will proceed in the direction for which the difference between the two half-reaction potentials is positive. This direction is the same as the direction of the more positive half-reaction.

General Plan for Solving Electrochemical Problems

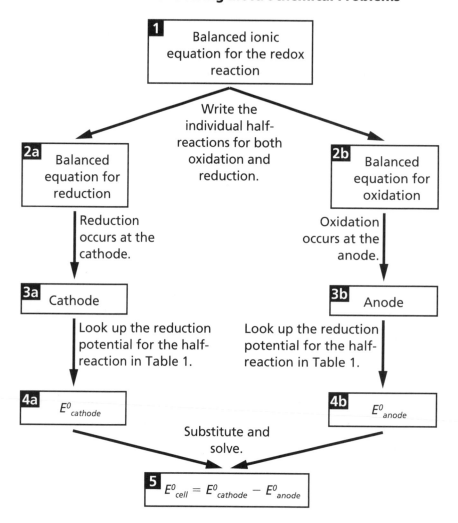

Sample Problem 1

Calculate the cell potential to determine whether the following reaction is spontaneous in the direction indicated.

$$Cd^{2+}(aq) + 2I^-(aq) \rightarrow Cd(s) + I_2(s)$$

Solution

ANALYZE

What is given in the problem?   **reactants and products**

What are you asked to find?   **whether the reaction is spontaneous**

Items	Data
Reactants	$Cd^{2+}(aq) + 2I^-(aq)$
Products	$Cd(s) + I_2(s)$
$E^0_{cathode}$	? V
E^0_{anode}	? V
E^0_{cell}	? V

PLAN

What steps are needed to determine whether the reaction is spontaneous?
Separate into oxidation and reduction half-reactions. Find reduction potentials for each. Solve the equation for the cell potential to determine if the reaction is spontaneous.

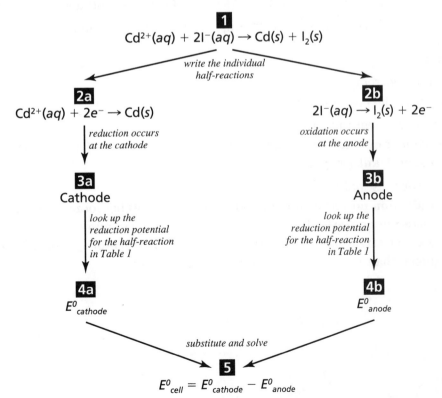

1
$Cd^{2+}(aq) + 2I^-(aq) \rightarrow Cd(s) + I_2(s)$

write the individual half-reactions

2a
$Cd^{2+}(aq) + 2e^- \rightarrow Cd(s)$

reduction occurs at the cathode

3a
Cathode

look up the reduction potential for the half-reaction in Table 1

4a
$E^0_{cathode}$

2b
$2I^-(aq) \rightarrow I_2(s) + 2e^-$

oxidation occurs at the anode

3b
Anode

look up the reduction potential for the half-reaction in Table 1

4b
E^0_{anode}

substitute and solve

5
$E^0_{cell} = E^0_{cathode} - E^0_{anode}$

Write the given equation.

$$Cd^{2+}(aq) + 2I^-(aq) \rightarrow Cd(s) + I_2(s)$$

The oxidation number of cadmium decreases; it is reduced.

$$Cd^{2+}(aq) + 2e^- \rightarrow Cd(s)$$

The oxidation number of iodine increases; it is oxidized.

$$2I^-(aq) \rightarrow I_2(s) + 2e^-$$

Cadmium is the cathode, and iodine is the anode.

$$E^0{}_{cathode} = \overset{from\ Table\ 1}{-0.40\ V}$$

$$E^0{}_{anode} = \overset{from\ Table\ 1}{+0.54\ V}$$

$$E^0{}_{cell} = \overset{given\ above}{E^0{}_{cathode}} - \overset{given\ above}{E^0{}_{anode}}$$

Determine spontaneity. If the cell potential is positive, the reaction is sponta-neous as written. If the cell potential is negative, the reaction is not spontaneous as written, but the reverse reaction is spontaneous.

COMPUTE

$$E^0{}_{cell} = -0.40\ V - 0.54\ V = -0.94\ V$$

The reaction potential is negative. Therefore, the reaction is not spontaneous. The reverse reaction would have a positive potential and would, therefore, be spontaneous.

$$Cd^{2+}(aq) + 2I^-(aq) \rightarrow Cd(s) + I_2(s)\ \text{not spontaneous}$$

$$Cd(s) + I_2(s) \rightarrow Cd^{2+}(aq) + 2I^-(aq)\ \text{spontaneous}$$

EVALUATE

Are the units correct?

Yes; cell potentials are in volts.

Is the number of significant figures correct?

Yes; the number of significant figures is correct because the half-cell potentials have two significant figures.

Is the answer reasonable?

Yes; the reduction potential for the half-reaction involving iodine was more positive than the potential for the reaction involving cadmium, which means that I_2 has a greater attraction for electrons than Cd^{2+}. Therefore, I_2 is more likely to be reduced than Cd^{2+}. The reverse reaction is favored.

Problem Solving *continued*

Practice

Use the reduction potentials in Table 1 to determine whether the following reactions are spontaneous as written. Report the E^0_{cell} for the reactions.

1. $Cu^{2+} + Fe \rightarrow Fe^{2+} + Cu$ **ans: +0.79 V; spontaneous**

2. $Pb^{2+} + Fe^{2+} \rightarrow Fe^{3+} + Pb$ **ans: −0.90 V; nonspontaneous**

3. $Mn^{2+} + 4H_2O + Sn^{2+} \rightarrow MnO_4^- + 8H^+ + Sn$ **ans: −1.64 V; nonspontaneous**

4. $MnO_4^{2-} + Cl_2 \rightarrow MnO_4^- + 2Cl^-$ **ans: +0.80 V; spontaneous**

| Problem Solving *continued*

5. $Hg_2^{2+} + 2MnO_4^{2-} \rightarrow 2Hg + 2MnO_4^{-}$ **ans: +0.24 V; spontaneous**

6. $2Li^+ + Pb \rightarrow 2Li + Pb^{2+}$ **ans: −2.91 V; nonspontaneous**

7. $Br_2 + 2Cl^- \rightarrow 2Br^- + Cl_2$ **ans: −0.29 V; nonspontaneous**

8. $S + 2I^- \rightarrow S^{2-} + I_2$ **ans: −1.02 V; nonspontaneous**

Problem Solving *continued*

Sample Problem 2

A cell is constructed in which the following two half-reactions can occur in either direction.

$$Zn^{2+} + 2e^- \rightleftarrows Zn$$

$$Br_2 + 2e^- \rightleftarrows 2Br^-$$

Write the full ionic equation for the cell in the spontaneous direction, identify the reactions occurring at the anode and cathode, and determine the cell's voltage.

Solution

ANALYZE

What is given in the problem?   **the reversible half-reactions of the cell**

What are you asked to find?   **the equation in the spontaneous direction; the voltage of the cell**

Items	Data
Half-reaction 1	$Zn^{2+} + 2e^- \rightleftarrows Zn$
Half-reaction 2	$Br_2 + 2e^- \rightleftarrows 2Br$
Reduction potential of 1	-0.76 V
Reduction potential of 2	$+1.07$ V
Full ionic reaction	?
Cell voltage	?

PLAN

What steps are needed to determine the spontaneous reaction of the cell and the cell voltage?

Determine which half-reaction has the more positive reduction potential. This will be the reduction half-reaction; it occurs at the cathode. Reverse the other half-reaction so that it becomes an oxidation half-reaction; it occurs at the anode. Adjust the half-reactions so that the same number of electrons are lost as are gained. Add the reactions together. Compute the cell voltage by the formula $E^0_{cell} = E^0_{cathode} - E^0_{anode}$, using the reduction potentials for the reaction at each electrode.

Problem Solving *continued*

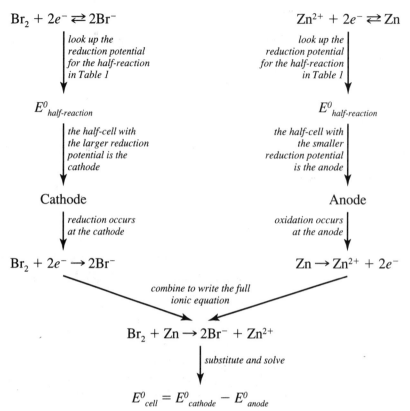

$$Br_2 + 2e^- \rightleftharpoons 2Br^- \qquad\qquad Zn^{2+} + 2e^- \rightleftharpoons Zn$$

look up the reduction potential for the half-reaction in Table 1 ⟶ *look up the reduction potential for the half-reaction in Table 1*

$$E^0_{half\text{-}reaction} \qquad\qquad E^0_{half\text{-}reaction}$$

the half-cell with the larger reduction potential is the cathode ⟶ *the half-cell with the smaller reduction potential is the anode*

Cathode Anode

reduction occurs at the cathode ⟶ *oxidation occurs at the anode*

$$Br_2 + 2e^- \rightarrow 2Br^- \qquad\qquad Zn \rightarrow Zn^{2+} + 2e^-$$

combine to write the full ionic equation

$$Br_2 + Zn \rightarrow 2Br^- + Zn^{2+}$$

substitute and solve

$$E^0_{cell} = E^0_{cathode} - E^0_{anode}$$

First, look up the reduction potentials for the two half-reactions in Table 1.

$$E^0_{Br_2} = \overset{\text{from Table 1}}{+1.07 \text{ V}}$$

$$E^0_{Zn} = \overset{\text{from Table 1}}{-0.76 \text{ V}}$$

Br_2 has the larger reduction potential; therefore, it is the cathode. Zn has the smaller reduction potential; therefore, it is the anode.

The cathode half-reaction is

$$Br_2 + 2e^- \rightarrow 2Br$$

The anode half-reaction is

$$Zn \rightarrow Zn^{2+} + 2e^-$$

The full-cell equation is

$$Br_2 + 2e^- \rightarrow 2Br^-$$
$$+ Zn \rightarrow Zn^{2+} + 2e^-$$
$$\overline{Br_2 + Zn \rightarrow 2Br^- + Zn^{2+}}$$

Substitute the reduction potentials for the anode and cathode into the cell potential equation, and solve the equation.

$$E^0_{cell} = E^0{}_{cathode}^{E^0_{Br_2}} - E^0{}_{anode}^{E^0_{Zn}}$$

| Problem Solving *continued*

COMPUTE

$$Br_2 + Zn \rightarrow 2Br^- + Zn^{2+}$$

$$E^0_{cell} = 1.07\ V - (-0.76\ V) = 1.83\ V$$

EVALUATE

Are the units correct?

Yes; the cell potential is in volts.

Is the number of significant figures correct?

Yes; the half-cell potentials were given to two decimal places.

Is the answer reasonable?

Yes; you would expect the reaction to have a positive cell potential because it should be spontaneous.

Practice

If a cell is constructed in which the following pairs of reactions are possible, what would be the cathode reaction, the anode reaction, and the overall cell voltage?

1. $Ca^{2+} + 2e^- \rightleftarrows Ca$
   $Fe^{3+} + 3e^- \rightleftarrows Fe$
   ans: cathode: $Fe^{3+} + 3e^- \rightarrow Fe$, anode: $Ca \rightarrow Ca^{2+} + 2e^-$, $E^0_{cell} = +2.83\ V$

2. $Ag^+ + e^- \rightleftarrows Ag$
   $S + 2H^+ + 2e^- \rightleftarrows H_2S$
   ans: cathode: $Ag^+ + e^- \rightarrow Ag$, anode: $H_2S \rightarrow S + 2H^+ + 2e^-$, $E^0_{cell} = +0.66\ V$

3. $Fe^{3+} + e^- \rightleftarrows Fe^{2+}$
   $Sn^{2+} + 2e^- \rightleftarrows Sn$
   ans: cathode: $Fe^{3+} + e^- \rightarrow Fe^{2+}$, anode: $Sn \rightarrow Sn^{2+} + 2e^-$, $E^0_{cell} = +0.91\ V$

4. $Cu^{2+} + 2e^- \rightleftarrows Cu$
   $Au^{3+} + 3e^- \rightleftarrows Au$
   ans: cathode: $Au^{3+} + 3e^- \rightarrow Au$, anode: $Cu \rightarrow Cu^{2+} + 2e^-$, $E^0_{cell} = +1.16\ V$

| Problem Solving *continued*

Additional Problems

Use reduction potentials to determine whether the reactions in the following 10 problems are spontaneous.

1. $Ba + Sn^{2+} \rightarrow Ba^{2+} + Sn$

2. $Ni + Hg^{2+} \rightarrow Ni^{2+} + Hg$

3. $2Cr^{3+} + 7H_2O + 6Fe^{3+} \rightarrow Cr_2O_7^{2-} + 14H^+ + 6Fe^{2+}$

4. $Cl_2 + Sn \rightarrow 2Cl^- + Sn^{2+}$

5. $Al + 3Ag^+ \rightarrow Al^{3+} + 3Ag$

6. $Hg_2^{2+} + S^{2-} \rightarrow 2Hg + S$

7. $Ba + 2Ag^+ \rightarrow Ba^{2+} + 2Ag$

8. $2I^- + Ca^{2+} \rightarrow I_2 + Ca$

9. $Zn + 2MnO_4^- \rightarrow Zn^{2+} + 2MnO_4^{2-}$

10. $2Cr^{3+} + 3Mg^{2+} + 7H_2O \rightarrow Cr_2O_7^{2-} + 14H^+ + 3Mg$

In the following problems, you are given a pair of reduction half-reactions. If a cell were constructed in which the pairs of half-reactions were possible, what would be the balanced equation for the overall cell reaction that would occur? Write the half-reactions that occur at the cathode and anode, and calculate the cell voltage.

11. $Cl_2 + 2e^- \rightleftarrows 2Cl^-$
$Ni^{2+} + 2e^- \rightleftarrows Ni$

12. $Fe^{3+} + 3e^- \rightleftarrows Fe$
$Hg^{2+} + 2e^- \rightleftarrows Hg$

13. $MnO_4^- + e^- \rightleftarrows MnO_4^{2-}$
$Al^{3+} + 3e^- \rightleftarrows Al$

14. $MnO_4^- + 8H^+ + 5e^- \rightleftarrows Mn^{2+} + 4H_2O$
$S + 2H^+ + 2e^- \rightleftarrows H_2S$

15. $Ca^{2+} + 2e^- \rightleftarrows Ca$
$Li^+ + e^- \rightleftarrows Li$

16. $Br_2 + 2e^- \rightleftarrows 2Br^-$
$MnO_4^- + 8H^+ + 5e^- \rightleftarrows Mn^{2+} + 4H_2O$

17. $Sn^{2+} + 2e^- \rightleftarrows Sn$
$Fe^{3+} + e^- \rightleftarrows Fe^{2+}$

18. $Zn^{2+} + 2e^- \rightleftarrows Zn$
$Cr_2O_7^{2-} + 14H^+ + 6e^- \rightleftarrows 2Cr^{3+} + 7H_2O$

19. $Ba^{2+} + 2e^- \rightleftarrows Ba$
$Ca^{2+} + 2e^- \rightleftarrows Ca$

20. $Hg_2^{2+} + 2e^- \rightleftarrows 2Hg$
$Cd^{2+} + 2e^- \rightleftarrows Cd$

Assessment

Quiz

Section: Oxidation-Reduction Reactions

In the space provided, write the letter of the term or phrase that best answers each question.

_____ **1.** What is the oxidation half-reaction for the following redox reaction?
$Zn + HgO \rightarrow ZnO + Hg$.
   a. $Zn \rightarrow Zn^{2+} + 2e^-$
   b. $Hg^{2+} + 2e^- \rightarrow Hg$
   c. $Zn + HgO$
   d. $ZnO + Hg$

_____ **2.** What is the reduction half-reaction for the following redox reaction?
$Zn + HgO \rightarrow ZnO + Hg$.
   a. $Zn \rightarrow Zn^{2+} + 2e^-$
   b. $Hg^{2+} + 2e^- \rightarrow Hg$
   c. $Zn + HgO$
   d. $ZnO + Hg$

_____ **3.** The oxidation number of oxygen atoms in compounds is usually
   a. 0.
   b. -1.
   c. -2.
   d. $+1$.

_____ **4.** The part of a reaction that involves only oxidation or reduction is
   a. a redox reaction.
   b. a reduction reaction.
   c. an oxidation-reduction equation.
   d. a half-reaction.

_____ **5.** The sum of the oxidation numbers for all atoms in a polyatomic ion is equal to
   a. -2.
   b. zero.
   c. the charge on that ion.
   d. the charge of the products.

_____ **6.** The sum of the oxidation numbers for all the atoms in a molecule is equal to
   a. -2.
   b. zero.
   c. the charge on that ion.
   d. the charge of the products.

| Quiz *continued*

_____ **7.** Substances that accept electrons easily and are reduced are called
   a. oxidizing agents.
   b. reducing agents.
   c. half-reactions.
   d. oxidation number.

_____ **8.** Metals, hydrogen, and carbon are common ____ and are oxidized.
   a. oxidizing agents
   b. reducing agents
   c. half-reactions
   d. oxidation numbers

_____ **9.** If oxidation is taking place, what also must be occurring?
   a. electroplating
   b. corrosion
   c. electrolysis
   d. reduction

_____ **10.** Another name for an oxidation-reduction reaction is
   a. oxidizing agent.
   b. redox reaction.
   c. reducing agent.
   d. half-reaction.

Assessment

Quiz

Section: Introduction to Electrochemistry

In the space provided, write the letter of the term or phrase that best answers each question.

_____ **1.** Electrochemistry is the study of the relationship between electric forces and
  a. physical reactions.
  b. chemical reactions.
  c. gravitational forces.
  d. electrode reactions.

_____ **2.** The voltage of an ordinary flashlight battery is 1.5 volts. If your flashlight takes three batteries placed end-to-end, what is the overall voltage driving electrons in the flashlight?
  a. 1.5 V
  b. 3.0 V
  c. 4.5 V
  d. 6.0 V

_____ **3.** An electrochemical cell consists of two electrodes separated by
  a. an anode.
  b. a cathode.
  c. a voltage.
  d. an electrolyte.

_____ **4.** Electrons are generated at the
  a. anode.
  b. cathode.
  c. circuit.
  d. electrolyte.

_____ **5.** What is used to keep two half-cells apart, but allows charges to flow?
  a. an electrolyte
  b. a cathode
  c. a porous barrier
  d. an anode

_____ **6.** Where does oxidation take place in an electrochemical cell?
  a. the anode
  b. the cathode
  c. the anode or the cathode
  d. the half-cell

Quiz *continued*

_____ **7.** The oxidation number in an anode reaction
   a. decreases.
   b. increases.
   c. does not change.
   d. None of the above

_____ **8.** The oxidation number in a cathode reaction
   a. decreases.
   b. increases.
   c. does not change.
   d. None of the above

_____ **9.** In an electrochemical cell, the cathode is the
   a. neutral electrode.
   b. electrode at which matter can gain or lose electrons.
   c. electrode at which matter gains electrons.
   d. electrode at which matter loses electrons.

_____ **10.** In an electrochemical cell, the anode is the
   a. neutral electrode.
   b. electrode at which matter can gain or lose electrons.
   c. electrode at which matter gains electrons.
   d. electrode at which matter loses electrons.

Assessment

Quiz

Section: Galvanic Cells

In the space provided, write the letter of the term or phrase that best answers each question.

_____ **1.** An electrochemical cell that generates energy is a(n)
    a. galvanic cell.
    b. electrolytic cell.
    c. electroplating cell.
    d. None of the above

_____ **2.** Electrons in a galvanic cell normally flow
    a. from cathode to anode.
    b. from anode to cathode.
    c. through a porous barrier.
    d. in both directions through an external circuit.

_____ **3.** For an electric current to exist in a galvanic cell, the two half-cells must be
    a. connected to a dry cell.
    b. in the same solution.
    c. completely isolated from one another.
    d. connected by a wire and a porous barrier.

_____ **4.** When a car battery is charging,
    a. electrical energy is converted into energy of motion.
    b. energy of motion is converted into electrical energy.
    c. chemical energy is converted into electrical energy.
    d. electrical energy is converted into chemical energy.

_____ **5.** When a car battery is discharging,
    a. electrical energy is converted into energy of motion.
    b. energy of motion is converted into electrical energy.
    c. chemical energy is converted into electrical energy.
    d. electrical energy is converted into chemical energy.

_____ **6.** As a metal corrodes, what happens to oxygen?
    a. It is reduced.
    b. It is oxidized.
    c. It turns into a metal.
    d. No changes are made.

| Quiz *continued*

_____ **7.** Corrosion is the disintegration of metals through
  a. combustion.
  b. reduction.
  c. oxidation.
  d. exposure.

_____ **8.** Which of the following best describes the corrosion cell formed when iron is placed in moist air?
  a. Iron becomes both the anode and the cathode.
  b. Salts dissolved in water are the cathode and iron is the anode.
  c. Oxygen and water form hydroxide ions that dissolve the iron.
  d. At the cathode, oxygen and water form hydroxide ions and at the anode the iron becomes iron ions.

TABLE 1 STANDARD ELECTRODE POTENTIALS

Electrode reaction	E^{o}(V)
$Al^{3+}(aq) + 3e^{-} \rightleftarrows Al(s)$	-1.66
$Zn^{2+}(aq) + 2e^{-} \rightleftarrows Zn(s)$	-0.7618
$Fe^{2+}(aq) + 2e^{-} \rightleftarrows Fe(s)$	-0.447
$Pb^{2+}(aq) + 2e^{-} \rightleftarrows Pb(s)$	-0.1262
$Fe^{3+}(aq) + 3e^{-} \rightleftarrows Fe(s)$	-0.037
$Cu^{2+}(aq) + 2e^{-} \rightleftarrows Cu(s)$	$+0.3419$
$Ag^{+}(aq) + e^{-} \rightleftarrows Ag(s)$	$+0.7996$

_____ **9.** From the values given in **Table 1,** which metal is most likely to be oxidized?
  a. Zn
  b. Ag
  c. Pb
  d. Cu

_____ **10.** Use **Table 1** to determine which of the following would protect iron best.
  a. Zn
  b. Ag
  c. Pb
  d. Cu

Assessment

Quiz

Section: Electrolytic Cells

In the space provided, write the letter of the term or phrase that best answers each question.

_____ 1. In which cell does a current drive a nonspontaneous redox reaction?
   a. electrolytic cell
   b. dry cell
   c. fuel cell
   d. galvanic cell

_____ 2. In an electrolytic cell, reduction occurs
   a. at the cathode.
   b. at the anode.
   c. at either the cathode or the anode.
   d. in the space between the cathode and the anode.

_____ 3. Which process deposits metal onto a surface?
   a. corrosion
   b. electroplating
   c. auto-oxidation
   d. oxidation

_____ 4. Electroplating is an application of which reactions?
   a. electrolytic reactions
   b. fuel cell reactions
   c. auto-oxidation reactions
   d. galvanic reactions

_____ 5. Electrical energy is converted into chemical energy within a(n)
   a. fuel cell.
   b. galvanic cell.
   c. half-cell.
   d. electrolytic cell.

_____ 6. When electrical energy is provided to a rechargeable cell from an external source, the cell acts as a(n)
   a. fuel cell.
   b. electrolytic cell.
   c. galvanic cell.
   d. half-cell.

Quiz *continued*

_____ **7.** The use of electrical energy to decompose a compound into its elements is called
  a. electroplating.
  b. corrosion.
  c. a half-reaction.
  d. electrolysis.

_____ **8.** Which element is obtained from the electrolysis of bauxite?
  a. hydrogen
  b. sodium
  c. aluminum
  d. carbon

_____ **9.** A major benefit of electroplating is that it
  a. creates concentrations of toxic materials that then need to be disposed of.
  b. protects metals from corrosion.
  c. saves time.
  d. leads to a buildup of impurities.

_____**10.** A major concern about electroplating is that it
  a. creates concentrations of toxic materials that then need to be disposed of.
  b. protects metals from corrosion
  c. improves the appearance of an object.
  d. can reduce the price of some items.

Assessment

Chapter Test

Oxidation, Reduction, and Electrochemistry

In the space provided, write the letter of the term or phrase that best completes each statement or best answers each question.

_____ 1. During oxidation, one or more electrons are removed from a substance, which increases its
  a. size.
  b. mass.
  c. valence.
  d. oxidation number.

_____ 2. The oxidation number of fluorine in a compound is always
  a. 0.
  b. -1.
  c. $+1$.
  d. $+2$.

_____ 3. The half-reaction that occurs at the cathode in the electrolysis of molten sodium bromide is
  a. $2Br^- \rightarrow Br_2 + 2e^-$.
  b. $Br_2 + 2e^- \rightarrow 2Br^-$.
  c. $Na^+ + e^- \rightarrow Na$.
  d. $Na \rightarrow Na^+ + e^-$.

_____ 4. The movement of electrons or other charged particles is described as
  a. electric potential.
  b. electric current.
  c. voltage.
  d. an electrode reaction.

_____ 5. In any electrochemical cell, the cathode is always the
  a. positive electrode.
  b. negative electrode.
  c. electrode at which matter gains electrons.
  d. electrode at which matter loses electrons.

_____ 6. In any electrochemical cell, the anode is always the
  a. positive electrode.
  b. negative electrode.
  c. electrode at which matter gains electrons.
  d. electrode at which matter loses electrons.

| **Chapter Test** *continued*

_____ **7.** In the reaction
$$Cu + NO_3^- + H_3O^+ \rightarrow Cu^{2+} + NO + H_2O$$
the coefficients of the balanced equation are
  a. 1,2,2,1,1,1.
  b. 4,3,2,4,3,1.
  c. 6,1,2,6,1,1.
  d. 3,2,8,3,2,12.

_____ **8.** Batteries are examples of which of the following?
  a. electrolytic cells
  b. galvanic cells
  c. equilibrium cells
  d. None of the above

_____ **9.** A corrosion cell is actually a type of
  a. redox reaction.
  b. electrode.
  c. galvanic cell.
  d. electrolytic cell.

_____ **10.** Which conditions make corrosion worse?
  a. airborne salt from the oceans
  b. salt spread on icy roads
  c. air pollutants
  d. All of the above

_____ **11.** To protect steel from corrosion, it is better to coat steel with another metal that
  a. does not corrode.
  b. is expensive.
  c. does corrode.
  d. is more durable.

_____ **12.** A voltmeter allows no current into a cell during measurements, meaning that the cell is
  a. galvanic.
  b. electrolytic.
  c. at equilibrium.
  d. unstable.

_____ **13.** What can electrode potentials predict about a half-reaction?
  a. the direction the reaction takes
  b. the voltage of the reaction
  c. the products of a reaction
  d. the reactants of the reaction

Chapter Test *continued*

_____**14.** What type of cell generates electrical energy?
    a. electrolytic cells
    b. electroplating cells
    c. galvanic cells
    d. oxidation cells

_____**15.** What type of cell consumes electrical energy?
    a. electrolytic cells
    b. fuel cells
    c. galvanic cells
    d. oxidation cells

_____**16.** What is needed to create chemical changes in an electrolytic cell?
    a. gravity
    b. high temperatures
    c. electricity
    d. a fuel cell

_____**17.** What type of overall reaction occurs in an electrolytic cell?
    a. a nonspontaneous reaction
    b. a spontaneous reaction
    c. an electrode reaction
    d. a nuclear reaction

_____**18.** The electrolysis of water results in
    a. purified drinking water.
    b. separate elements of hydrogen and oxygen.
    c. the formation of an electrolyte.
    d. unsafe drinking water.

_____**19.** Aluminum is obtained first from
    a. recycling soda cans.
    b. pure sodium chloride.
    c. bauxite.
    d. the electrolysis of water.

_____**20.** Electroplating is coating a material with
    a. a plastic covering.
    b. bauxite.
    c. another metal.
    d. reducing agents.

| Chapter Test *continued*

Answer the following questions in the spaces provided.

21. Explain the difference between electrolytic and galvanic cells.

_____

_____

_____

_____

22. What features are common to all batteries? Explain your answer.

_____

_____

_____

23. Why must reduction always be accompanied by oxidation?

_____

_____

_____

Answer the following problems in the spaces provided.

TABLE 1: STANDARD ELECTRODE POTENTIALS

Electrode reaction	$E°$(V)
$2H_3O^+(aq) + 2e^- \rightleftarrows H_2(g) + 2H_2O(l)$	0.0000
$Cu^{2+}(aq) + e^- \rightleftarrows Cu^+(aq)$	+0.15
$Cu^{2+}(aq) + 2e^- \rightleftarrows Cu(s)$	+0.3419
$Ag^+(aq) + e^- \rightleftarrows Ag(s)$	+0.7996

24. Refer to Table 1. What is the voltage of the cell for the following reaction?

$$Cu + 2AgNO_3 \rightarrow 2Ag + Cu(NO_3)_2$$

25. A certain electrochemical cell has $Zn + HgO \rightarrow ZnO + Hg$ for its cell reaction. Write the reaction that is occurring at each electrode.

Anode: **Cathode:**

Name _____ Class _____ Date _____

Quick Lab

Listen Up

OBJECTIVE

Create a simple galvanic cell.

MATERIALS

For each group of 2–4 students:

- alligator clips (2)
- copper strip
- earphone
- raw potato
- zinc strip

Always wear safety goggles and a lab apron to protect your eyes and clothing. If you get a chemical in your eyes, immediately flush the chemical out at the eyewash station while calling to your teacher. Know the location of the emergency lab shower and eyewash station and the procedures for using them.

Procedure

1. Press a zinc strip and a copper strip into a raw potato. The strips should be about 0.5 cm apart but should not touch one another.

2. While listening to the earphone, touch one wire from the earphone to one of the metal strips and the other wire from the earphone to the second metal strip using alligator clips. Record your observations.

3. While listening to the earphone, touch both wires to a single metal strip. Record your observations.

Analysis

1. Compare your results from step 2 with your results from step 3. Suggest an explanation for any similarities or differences.

_____

_____

_____

_____

2. Suggest an explanation for the sound.

_____

_____

Inquiry Lab

Redox Titration: Mining Feasibility Study

May 11, 2003

George Taylor, Director of Analysis

CheMystery Labs, Inc.

52 Fulton Street

Springfield, VA 22150

Dear Mr. Taylor:

Because of the high quality of your firm's work in the past, Goldstake is again asking that you submit a bid for a mining feasibility study. A study site in New Mexico has yielded some promising iron ore deposits, and we are evaluating the potential yield.

Your bid should include the cost of evaluating the sample we are sending with this letter and the fees for 20 additional analyses to be completed over the next year. The sample is a slurry extracted from the mine using a special process that converts the iron ore into iron(II) sulfate, $FeSO_4$, dissolved in water. The mine could produce up to 1.0×10^5 L of this slurry daily, but we need to know how much iron is in that amount of slurry before we proceed.

The contract for the other analyses will be awarded based on the accuracy of this analysis and the quality of the report. Your report will be used for two purposes: to evaluate the site for quantity of iron and to determine who our analytical consultant will be if the site is developed into a mining operation. I look forward to reviewing your bid proposal.

Sincerely,

Lynn L. Brown

Director of Operations

Goldstake Mining Company

References

Review more information on redox reactions. Remember to add a small amount of sulfuric acid, H_2SO_4, so that the iron will stay in the Fe^{2+} form. Calculate your disposal costs based on the mass of potassium permanganate, $KMnO_4$, and iron(II) sulfate, $FeSO_4$ in your solutions, as well as the mass of the H_2SO_4 solution.

Redox Titration: Mining Feasibility Study *continued*

Memorandum

Date: May 12, 2003

To: Crystal Sievers

From: George Taylor

Good news! The quality of our work has earned us a repeat customer, Goldstake Mining Company. This analysis could turn into a long-term contract. Perform the analysis more than one time so that we can be confident of our accuracy.

Before you begin your analysis, send Ms. Brown the following items:

- a detailed, one-page plan for the procedure and all necessary data tables

- a detailed sheet that lists all of the equipment and materials you plan to use

When you have completed the laboratory work, please prepare a report in the form of a two-page letter to Ms. Brown. Include the following information:

- moles and grams of $FeSO_4$ in 10 mL of sample

- moles, grams, and percentage of iron(II) in 10 mL of the sample

- the number of kilograms of iron that the company could extract from the mine each year, assuming that 1.0×10^5 L of slurry could be mined per day, year round

- a balanced equation for the redox equation

- a detailed and organized data and analysis section showing calculations of how you determined the moles, grams, and percentage of iron(II) in the sample (include calculations of the mean, or average, of the multiple trials)

Redox Titration: Mining Feasibility Study *continued*

 Scissors (pins) are sharp; use with care to avoid cutting yourself or others.

Do not heat glassware that is broken, chipped, or cracked. Use tongs or a hot mitt to handle heated glassware and other equipment because hot glassware does not always look hot.

When using a Bunsen burner, confine long hair and loose clothing. If your clothing catches on fire, WALK to the emergency lab shower and use it to put out the fire. Do not heat glassware that is broken, chipped, or cracked. Use tongs or a hot mitt to handle heated glassware and other equipment because hot glassware does not always look hot.

When heating a substance in a test tube, the mouth of the test tube should point away from where you and others are standing. Watch the test tube at all times to prevent the contents from boiling over.

Do not touch any chemicals. If you get a chemical on your skin or clothing, wash the chemical off at the sink while calling to your teacher. Make sure you carefully read the labels and follow the precautions on all containers of chemicals that you use. If there are no precautions stated on the label, ask your teacher what precautions to follow. Do not taste any chemicals or items used in the laboratory. Never return leftovers to their original container; take only small amounts to avoid wasting supplies.

Always wear safety goggles and a lab apron to protect your eyes and clothing. If you get a chemical in your eyes, immediately flush the chemical out at the eyewash station while calling to your teacher. Know the location of the emergency lab shower and eyewash station and the procedures for using them.

Skills Practice Lab

Redox Titration

You are a chemist working for a chemical analysis firm. A large pharmaceutical company has hired you to help salvage some products that were damaged by a small fire in their warehouse. Although there was only minimal smoke and fire damage to the warehouse and products, the sprinkler system ruined the labeling on many of the pharmaceuticals. The firm's best-selling products are iron tonics used to treat low-level anemia. The tonics are produced from hydrated iron(II) sulfate, $FeSO_4 \cdot 7H_2O$. The different types of tonics contain different concentrations of $FeSO_4$. You have been hired to help the pharmaceutical company figure out the proper label for each bottle of tonic.

In the chapter "Acids and Bases" you studied acid-base titrations in which an unknown amount of acid is titrated with a carefully measured amount of base. In this procedure a similar approach called a redox titration is used. In a redox titration, the reducing agent, Fe^{2+}, is oxidized to Fe^{3+} by the oxidizing agent, MnO_4^-. When this process occurs, the Mn in MnO_4^- changes from a $+7$ to a $+2$ oxidation state and has a noticeably different color. You can use this color change in the same way that you used the color change of phenolphthalein in acid-base titrations—to signify a redox reaction end point. When the reaction is complete, any excess MnO_4^- added to the reaction mixture will give the solution a pink or purple color. The volume data from the titration, the known molarity of the $KMnO_4$ solution, and the mole ratio from the following balanced redox equation will give you the information you need to calculate the molarity of the $FeSO_4$ solution.

$$5Fe^{2+}(aq) + MnO_4^-(aq) + 8H^+(aq) \rightarrow 5Fe^{3+}(aq) + Mn^{2+}(aq) + 4H_2O(l)$$

To determine how to label the bottles, you must determine the concentration of iron(II) ions in the sample from an unlabeled bottle from the warehouse by answering the following questions:

- How can the volume data obtained from the titration and the mole ratios from the balanced redox reaction be used to determine the concentration of the sample?

- Which tonic is in the sample, given information about the concentration of each tonic?

OBJECTIVES

Demonstrate proficiency in performing redox titrations and recognizing the end point of a redox reaction.

Determine the concentration of a solution using stoichiometry and volume data from a titration.

| Redox Titration *continued*

MATERIALS

- beaker, 250 mL (2)
- beaker, 400 mL
- burets (2)
- distilled water
- double buret clamp
- Erlenmeyer flask, 125 mL (4)

- $FeSO_4$ solution
- graduated cylinder, 100 mL
- H_2SO_4, 1.0 M
- $KMnO_4$, 0.0200 M
- ring stand
- wash bottle

 Always wear safety goggles, gloves, and a lab apron to protect your eyes and clothing. If you get a chemical in your eyes, immediately flush the chemical out at the eyewash station while calling to your teacher. Know the location of the emergency lab shower and eyewash station and the procedures for using them.

 Do not touch any chemicals. If you get a chemical on your skin or clothing, wash the chemical off at the sink while calling to your teacher. Make sure you carefully read the labels and follow the precautions on all containers of chemicals that you use. If there are no precautions stated on the label, ask your teacher what precautions to follow. Do not taste any chemicals or items used in the laboratory. Never return leftovers to their original container; take only small amounts to avoid wasting supplies.

Call your teacher in the event of a spill. Spills should be cleaned up promptly, according to your teacher's directions.

Acids and bases are corrosive. If an acid or base spills onto your skin or clothing, wash the area immediately with running water. Call your teacher in the event of an acid spill. Acid or base spills should be cleaned up promptly.

Never put broken glass in a regular waste container. Broken glass should be disposed of separately according to your teacher's instructions.

| Redox Titration *continued*

Procedure

1. Put on safety goggles, gloves, and a lab apron.

2. Clean two 50 mL burets with a buret brush and distilled water. Rinse each buret at least three times with distilled water to remove any contaminants.

3. Label two 250 mL beakers "0.0200 M $KMnO_4$," and "$FeSO_4$ solution." Label three of the flasks 1, 2, and 3. Label the 400 mL beaker "Waste." Label one buret "$KMnO_4$" and the other "$FeSO_4$."

4. Measure approximately 75 mL of 0.0200 M $KMnO_4$, and pour it into the appropriately labeled beaker. Obtain approximately 75 mL of $FeSO_4$ solution, and pour it into the appropriately labeled beaker.

5. Rinse one buret three times with a few milliliters of 0.0200 M $KMnO_4$ from the appropriately labeled beaker. Collect these rinses in the waste beaker. Rinse the other buret three times with small amounts of $FeSO_4$ solution from the appropriately labeled beaker. Collect these rinses in the waste beaker.

6. Set up the burets. Fill one buret with approximately 50 mL of the 0.0200 M $KMnO_4$ from the beaker, and fill the other buret with approximately 50 mL of the $FeSO_4$ solution from the other beaker.

7. With the waste beaker underneath its tip, open the $KMnO_4$ buret long enough to be sure the buret tip is filled. Repeat for the $FeSO_4$ buret.

8. Add 50 mL of distilled water to one of the 125 mL Erlenmeyer flasks, and add one drop of 0.0200 M $KMnO_4$ to the flask. Set this aside to use as a color standard to compare with the titration and to determine the end point.

9. Record the initial buret readings for both solutions in your data table. Add 10.0 mL of the hydrated iron(II) sulfate, $FeSO_4 \cdot 7H_2O$, solution to flask 1. Add 5 mL of 1.0 M H_2SO_4 to the $FeSO_4$ solution in this flask. The acid will help keep the Fe^{2+} ions in the reduced state, allowing you time to titrate.

10. Slowly add $KMnO_4$ from the buret to the $FeSO_4$ in the flask while swirling the flask. When the color of the solution matches the color standard you prepared in step **8,** record the final readings of the burets in your data table.

11. Empty the titration flask into the waste beaker. Repeat the titration procedure in steps **9** and **10** with flasks 2 and 3.

12. Always clean up the lab and all equipment after use. Dispose of the contents of the waste beaker in the container designated by your teacher. Also pour the contents of the color-standard flask into this container. Wash your hands thoroughly after cleaning up the area and equipment.

| Redox Titration *continued*

TABLE 1 TITRATION DATA

Trial	Initial KmnO$_4$ volume	Final KMnO$_4$ volume	Initial FeSO$_4$ volume	Final FeSO$_4$ volume
1				
2				
3				

Analysis

1. Analyzing Data Calculate the number of moles of MnO_4^- reduced in each trial.

   Trial 1:

   Trial 2:

   Trial 3:

2. Analyzing Data Calculate the number of moles of Fe^{2+} oxidized in each trial.

   Trial 1:

   Trial 2:

   Trial 3:

3. Analyzing Data Calculate the average concentration (molarity) of the iron tonic.

Redox Titration *continued*

4. **Explaining Events** Explain why it was important to rinse the burets with $KMnO_4$ or $FeSO_4$ before adding the solutions. (Hint: Consider what would happen to the concentration of each solution if it were added to a buret that had been rinsed only with distilled water.)

_____

_____

_____

_____

_____

Conclusions

5. **Evaluating Data** The company makes three different types of iron tonics: Feravide A, with a concentration of 0.145 M $FeSO_4$; Feravide Extra-Strength, with 0.225 M $FeSO_4$; and Feravide Jr., with 0.120 M $FeSO_4$. Which tonic is your sample?

_____

_____

6. **Evaluating Methods** What possible sources of error can you identify with this procedure? If you can think of ways to eliminate them, ask your teacher to approve your plan, and run the procedure again.

_____

_____

_____

_____

Extensions

1. **Research and Communication** Blueprints are based on a photochemical reaction. The paper is treated with a solution of iron(III) ammonium citrate and potassium hexacyanoferrate(III) and dried in the dark. When a tracing-paper drawing is placed on the blueprint paper and exposed to light, Fe^{3+} ions are reduced to Fe^{2+} ions, which react with hexacyanoferrate(III) ions in the moist paper to form the blue color on the paper. The lines of the drawing block the light and prevent the reduction of Fe^{3+} ions, resulting in white lines. Find out how sepia prints are made, and report on this information.

_____

_____

_____

_____

2. **Building Models** Electrochemical cells are based on the process of electron flow in a system with varying potential differences. Batteries are composed of such systems and contain different chemicals for different purposes and price ranges. You can make simple experimental batteries using metal wires and items such as lemons, apples, and potatoes. What are some other "home-made" battery sources, and what is the role of these food items in producing electrical energy that can be measured as battery power? Explain your answers.

_____

_____

_____

_____

_____

Skills Practice Lab

Electroplating for Corrosion Protection

SITUATION

Your company has been contacted by a manufacturer of electrical circuits. The company uses 1.0 M HCl to clean newly manufactured circuits. They've decided to store the acid in large metal tanks instead of reagent bottles. The company has narrowed down the choices to copper, zinc-plated copper, and iron-plated copper. You have been asked to evaluate these choices.

BACKGROUND

Solutions of acids can oxidize some metals. The displacement reaction of magnesium and hydrochloric acid is an example.

$$\underset{0}{Mg(s)} + \underset{+1-1}{2HCl(aq)} \longrightarrow \underset{+2\ -1}{MgCl_2(aq)} + \underset{0}{H_2(g)}$$

Metals that react can be electroplated with a thin layer of a less reactive metal. In an electroplating cell, electrical energy is used to reduce metal ions in solution, causing it to adhere to the surface of an object functioning as an anode. **Figure 1** shown here summarizes the apparatus and the process.

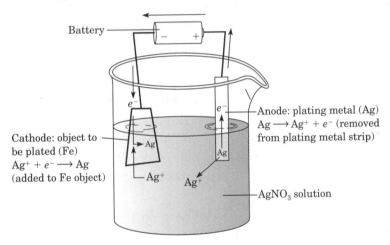

Figure 1

PROBLEM

You must first prepare samples of the plated metals. Then you must test each one in 1.0 M HCl to determine which resists corrosion the best.

OBJECTIVES

Construct an electrolytic cell with an electrolyte, two electrodes, and a battery.

Use the electrolytic cell to plate one metal onto another.

Test the plated metals and a sample of the original metal to determine how well they resist corrosion by an acidic solution.

Relate the results to the activity series and to standard reduction potentials.

Electroplating for Corrosion Protection *continued*

MATERIALS

- balance
- battery, 6 V (lantern type)
- beaker, 400 mL
- beakers, 150 mL (3)
- copper wire, 10 cm lengths (3)
- distilled water
- $FeCl_3$ plating solution
- gloves
- HCl, 1.0 M
- iron strip, 1 cm $\times$ 8 cm
- lab apron
- safety goggles
- steel wool

- stick-on label
- stopwatch or clock with second hand
- test-tube rack
- test tubes, large (3)
- wax pencil
- wire with alligator clips (2 pieces)
- zinc strip, 1 cm $\times$ 8 cm
- $ZnSO_4$ plating solution

Optional equipment
- beaker tongs
- drying oven

 Always wear safety goggles, gloves, and a lab apron to protect your eyes and clothing. If you get a chemical in your eyes, immediately flush the chemical out at the eyewash station while calling to your teacher. Know the location of the emergency lab shower and eyewash station and the procedures for using them.

 Do not touch any chemicals. If you get a chemical on your skin or clothing, wash the chemical off at the sink while calling to your teacher. Make sure you carefully read the labels and follow the precautions on all containers of chemicals that you use. If there are no precautions stated on the label, ask your teacher what precautions to follow. Do not taste any chemicals or items used in the laboratory. Never return leftovers to their original container; take only small amounts to avoid wasting supplies.

Call your teacher in the event of a spill. Spills should be cleaned up promptly, according to your teacher's directions.

Acids and bases are corrosive. If an acid or base spills onto your skin or clothing, wash the area immediately with running water. Call your teacher in the event of an acid spill. Acid or base spills should be cleaned up promptly.

Do not heat glassware that is broken, chipped, or cracked. Use tongs or a hot mitt to handle heated glassware and other equipment because hot glassware does not always look hot.

Electroplating for Corrosion Protection *continued*

PART 1–PREPARATION

1. Put on safety goggles, gloves, and a lab apron.

2. Label two of the 150 mL beakers *FeCl₃* and *ZnSO₄*. Label the 400 mL beaker *Waste*.

3. Make loops on one end of each of the wires. Using a piece of a stick-on label, label the wires *Cu*, *Fe/Cu*, and *Zn/Cu* just below the loops.

4. Polish each wire and metal strip with steel wool.

5. Using the laboratory balance, measure the mass of the *Fe/Cu* wire. Record it in your data table.

PART 2–PLATING

6. Attach one end of a wire with alligator clips to the loop on the *Fe/Cu* wire. Attach the alligator clip on the other end of the wire to the negative ($-$) terminal of the battery.

7. Attach one end of the other wire with alligator clips to the iron strip. Clip the other end of this wire to the positive ($+$) terminal of the battery, as shown in **Figure 2** below. Keep the iron strip away from the copper wire.

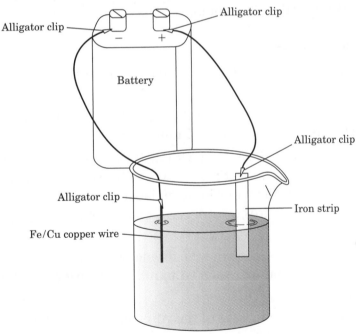

Figure 2

8. Pour 80 mL of the FeCl₃ solution into the *FeCl₃* beaker.

9. Using a stopwatch or clock with second hand to measure the time, immerse both the copper wire and the iron strip in the beaker, being careful to keep the alligator clips out of the solution. Use the loop to hang the wire on the beaker.

10. After about 5 min, remove the copper wire and the iron strip. Record the time elapsed to the nearest 1.0 s.

11. Rinse the *Fe/Cu* wire with distilled water, collecting the rinse water in the *Waste* beaker. Record your observations about the *Fe/Cu* wire in your data table.

12. Hold the unplated *Zn/Cu* wire close to the plated *Fe/Cu* wire. Use a wax pencil to make a mark on the *Zn/Cu* and *Cu* wires at about the same level as the edge of the plating on the *Fe/Cu* wire. Measure and record the masses of these wires.

13. Repeat steps **6–11** with the zinc metal strip, zinc sulfate solution in the *ZnSO₄* beaker, and the wire labeled *Zn/Cu*. Be certain to plate the wire for exactly the same amount of time. Also be certain that the *Zn/C*u wire is immersed up to the wax pencil mark.

14. Place the plated wires in the unlabeled 150 mL beaker so that they are not touching each other. Either allow the wires to dry in the beaker overnight, or place the beaker in a drying oven for 10 min. **Remember to use beaker tongs to handle all glassware that has been in the drying oven.**

15. After the wires have cooled, measure and record the masses of the *Fe/Cu* wire and the *Zn/Cu* wire in the data table.

16. In your data table rewrite the original mass of the *Cu* wire in the *New mass of wire (g)* row under the *Cu* column.

PART 3–TESTING REACTIVITY

17. Fill each of the test tubes about one-third full of 1.0 M HCl. Place the test tubes in a test-tube rack.

18. Place one of the wires into each of the test tubes so that only the plated parts are in the HCl solution. Wait about 5 min.

19. Remove the wires, and rinse them with distilled water, collecting the rinse in the *Waste* beaker. Record the time and your observations about the wires in your data table. Place the wires in the unlabeled 150 mL beaker so that they do not touch. Dry the wires overnight, or place them in a drying oven for 10 min.

20. Remove the beaker of wires from the drying oven and allow it to cool. **Remember to use beaker tongs to handle beakers that have been in the drying oven.**

21. Measure and record the masses of the wires in your data table as *Mass of wire after HCl (g)*.

22. Your teacher will provide separate disposal containers for each solution, each metal, and contents of the *Waste* beaker. The HCl from the test tubes can be poured into the same container as the contents of the *Waste* beaker.

Electroplating for Corrosion Protection *continued*

TABLE 1: ELECTROPLATING DATA

	Cu	Fe/Cu	Zn/Cu
Mass of wire (g)			
Plating time (s)			
New mass of wire (g)			
HCl time (s)			
Mass of wire after HCl (g)			

Observations

_____

_____

_____

_____

Analysis

1. Applying Models Write the equation for the half-reactions occurring on the metal strip and the copper wire in the $FeCl_3$ and $ZnSO_4$ beakers. Which is the anode in each one? Which is the cathode in each one?

_____

_____

_____

_____

2. Analyzing Data How many grams and moles of iron and zinc were plated onto the *Fe/Cu* and *Zn/Cu* wires?

Conclusions

3. Analyzing Results Which metal or metal combination was the least reactive in HCl? Explain the basis for your conclusion.

_____

_____

_____

4. Evaluating Conclusions What disadvantages relating to the use of the least reactive metal for the tanks can you think of?

_____

_____

_____

_____

Extensions

1. Research and Communication Find out what measures are taken to try to prevent metal bridges and buildings from corroding, and prepare a chart to show the different methods, their relative costs, and their general uses.

_____

_____

_____

_____

_____

_____

_____

_____

_____

Skills Practice Lab

PROBEWARE LAB

Micro-Voltaic Cells

Your small plane has just crashed on a remote island in the South Pacific. After recovering from the crash, you inventory the plane's contents. The only useful item still working in the plane is the radio, but the plane's battery has been completely destroyed, and you have no other means of powering the radio. Wandering around the island, you discover a small building that appears to be an abandoned research facility. Inside you discover a working gasoline generator and a laboratory filled with chemicals and various items of lab equipment, but no batteries. Upon careful consideration, you decide that there is no way to get the generator to the radio or the radio to the lab. You decide that your best bet is to construct a new battery.

In one of the cabinets, you discover a collection of metal strips and solutions. The writing is in a foreign language with which you are unfamiliar. It is apparent from the writing that certain metals correspond to certain solutions. Remembering a little about electrochemistry from your high school chemistry class, you decide that you can use the metal strips and solutions to build an electrochemical cell. You realize that before you can begin, you need to establish a table of reduction potentials in order to choose the proper metals for the anode and cathode of the cell. After further searching, you discover a working voltmeter and all the materials necessary to create a series of micro-voltaic cells using the unknown metals and solutions.

In this experiment, you will be using a calculator-interfaced voltage probe in place of a voltmeter. The (+) lead makes contact with one metal and the (−) lead with another. If a positive voltage appears on the calculator screen, the cell has been connected correctly. If the voltage reading is negative, switch the positions of the leads. The metal attached to the (+) lead is the cathode (where reduction takes place) and thus has a higher, more positive, reduction potential. The metal attached to the (−) lead is the anode (where oxidation takes place) and has the lower, more negative, reduction potential.

OBJECTIVES

- **Measure** potential differences between various pairs of half-cells.

- **Predict** potentials of half-cell combinations.

- **Compare** measured cell potentials with predicted cell potentials.

- **Calculate** percentage error for measured potentials.

- **Establish** the reduction potentials for five unknown metals.

| Micro-Voltaic Cells *continued*

MATERIALS

- filter paper, 11.0 cm diameter
- metals M_1, M_2, M_3, M_4, and M_5, 1×1 cm each
- $NaNO_3$, 1 M
- sandpaper
- solutions of M_1^{2+}, M_2^{2+}, . . . , and M_5^{2+}, 1 M each

EQUIPMENT

- forceps
- glass plate, 15×15 cm, or Petri dish, 11.5 cm diameter
- LabPro or CBL2 interface
- TI graphing calculator
- voltage probe

SAFETY

- Wear safety goggles when working around chemicals, acids, bases, flames, or heating devices.
- If any substance gets in your eyes, notify your instructor immediately and flush your eyes with running water for at least 15 minutes.
- If a chemical is spilled on the floor or lab bench, alert your instructor, but do not clean it up unless your instructor says it is OK to do so.
- Secure loose clothing, and remove dangling jewelry. Do not wear open-toed shoes or sandals in the lab.
- Wear an apron or lab coat to protect your clothing when working with chemicals.
- Never return unused chemicals to the original container; follow instructions for proper disposal.
- Always use caution when working with chemicals.
- Never mix chemicals unless specifically directed to do so.
- Never taste, touch, or smell chemicals unless specifically directed to do so.

Procedure

EQUIPMENT PREPARATION

1. Obtain and wear goggles.

2. Plug the voltage probe into Channel 1 of the LabPro or CBL 2 interface. Use the link cable to connect the TI graphing calculator to the interface. Firmly press in the cable ends.

3. Turn on the calculator, and start the DATAMATE program. Press [CLEAR] to reset the program.

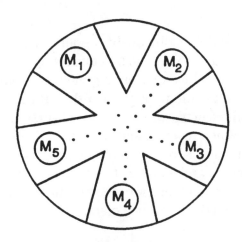

FIGURE 1

4. Set up the calculator and interface for the voltage probe.

a. If the calculator displays VOLTAGE (V) in CH 1, proceed directly to Step 5. If it does not, continue with this step to set up your sensor manually.

b. Select SETUP from the main screen.

c. Press [ENTER] to select CH 1.

d. Select the voltage probe you are using from the SELECT SENSOR menu.

e. Select OK to return to the main screen.

5. Obtain a piece of filter paper, and draw five small circles with connecting lines, as shown in **Figure 1**. Using a pair of scissors, cut wedges between the circles as shown. Label the circles M_1, M_2, M_3, M_4, and M_5. Place the filter paper on top of the glass plate.

6. Obtain five pieces of metal, "M_1," "M_2," "M_3," "M_4," and "M_5." Sand each piece of metal on both sides. Place each metal near the circle with the same number.

7. Place three drops of each solution on its circle (M_1^{2+} on M_1, etc.). Then place the piece of metal on the wet spot with its respective cation. The top side of the metal should be kept dry. Then add several drops of 1 M $NaNO_3$ to the line drawn between each circle and the center of the filter paper. Be sure there is a continuous trail of $NaNO_3$ between each circle and the center. You may have to periodically dampen the filter paper with $NaNO_3$ during the experiment. **CAUTION:** *Handle these solutions with care. Some are poisonous, and some cause hard-to-remove stains. If a spill occurs, ask your teacher how to clean it up safely.*

| Micro-Voltaic Cells *continued*

DATA COLLECTION

8. Use metal M_1 (the one that is obviously copper) as the reference metal. Determine the potential of four cells by connecting M_1 to M_2, M_1 to M_3, M_1 to M_4, and M_1 to M_5. This is done by bringing the (+) lead in contact with one metal and the (−) lead in contact with the other. If the voltage displayed on the main screen of the calculator is (−), then reverse the leads. Wait about five seconds to take a voltage reading, and record the (+) value appearing on the calculator screen in Table 1 (round to the nearest 0.01 V). Also record which metal is the (+) terminal and which is (−), when the voltage value is positive. Use the same procedure and measure the potential of the other three cells, continuing to use M_1 as the reference electrode.

DATA TABLE 1

Voltaic cell (metals used)	Measured potential (V)	Metal number of (+) lead	Metal number of (−) lead
M_1 / M_2			
M_1 / M_3			
M_1 / M_4			
M_1 / M_5			

9. Go to Step 1 of Processing the Data. Use the method described in Step 1 to rank the five metals from the lowest (−) reduction potential to the highest (+) reduction potential. Then *predict* the potentials for the remaining six cell combinations.

10. Now return to your work station and *measure* the potential of the six remaining half-cell combinations. If the $NaNO_3$ salt bridge solution has dried, you may have to re-moisten it. Record each measured potential in Table 2.

DATA TABLE 2

	Predicted potential (V)	Measured potential (V)	Percentage error (%)
M_2 / M_3			
M_2 / M_4			
M_2 / M_5			
M_3 / M_4			
M_3 / M_5			
M_4 / M_5			

11. When you are finished, select QUIT and exit the DATAMATE program.

12. When you have finished, use forceps to remove each of the pieces of metal from the filter paper. Rinse each piece of metal with tap water. Dry it, and return it to the correct container. Remove the filter paper from the glass plate using the forceps, and discard it as directed by your teacher. Rinse the glass plate with tap water, making sure that your hands do not come in contact with wet spots on the glass.

PROCESSING THE DATA

1. After finishing Step 8 in the procedure, arrange the five metals (including M_1) in Data Table 2 from the lowest reduction potential at the top (most negative) to the highest reduction potential at the bottom (most positive). Metal M_1, the standard reference, will be given an arbitrary value of 0.00 V. If the other metal was correctly connected to the *negative* terminal, it will be placed *above* M_1 in the chart (with a negative E° value). If it was connected to the positive terminal, it will be placed below M_1 in the chart (with a positive E° value). The numerical value of the potential relative to M_1 will simply be the value that you measured. Record your results in Table 3.

DATA TABLE 3

Metal (M_x)	Lowest (−) reduction potential, E° (V)
	Highest (+) reduction potential, E° (V)

Then calculate the *predicted* potential of each of the remaining cell combinations shown in Table 2, using the reduction potentials you just determined (in Table 3). Record the predicted cell potentials in Table 2. Return to Step 10 in the procedure, and finish the experiment.

2. Calculate the percentage error for each of the potentials you measured in Step 11 of the procedure. Do this by comparing the measured cell potentials with the predicted cell potentials in Table 2.

Analysis

1. Examining data Which metal had the highest reduction potential? Which had

the lowest reduction potential? _____

_____

_____

2. Examining data Which combination of metals had the largest measured cell

potential?_____

_____

_____

3. Analyzing results In Step 8 the metal M_1 was arbitrarily given a reduction
potential of 0.00 V and used as the reference metal in determining the potential of each voltaic cell. The metal M_1 can be positively identified as being
copper. According to the Table of Standard Reduction Potentials, Cu has a
reduction potential of +0.34 V. Adjust all of the reduction potentials in Table 3
by adding +0.34 V. Use the Table of Standard Reduction Potentials found in
your textbook to properly identify each of the unknown metals in Table 3.

Conclusions

1. Drawing conclusions If metal M_4 was actually gold, would your measured

cell potential had been higher or lower? Explain why. _____

_____

_____

_____

_____

2. Inferring conclusions If the battery back in the plane requires a 6 V power
source, how can you arrange the electrochemical cell to yield the necessary

voltage? _____

_____

_____

_____

_____

Lesson Plan

Section: Oxidation-Reduction Reactions

Pacing

Regular Schedule	**with lab(s):** 4 days	**without lab(s):** 2 days
Block Schedule	**with lab(s):** 2 days	**without lab(s):** 1 day

Objectives

1. Identify atoms that are oxidized or reduced through electron transfer.

2. Assign oxidation numbers to atoms in compounds and ions.

3. Identify redox reactions by analyzing changes in oxidation numbers for different atoms in the reaction.

4. Balance equations for oxidation-reduction reactions through the half-reaction method.

National Science Education Standards Covered

UNIFYING CONCEPTS AND PROCESSES

UCP 1 Systems, order, and organization

UCP 3 Change, constancy, and measurement

UCP 4 Evolution and equilibrium

PHYSICAL SCIENCE—CHEMICAL REACTIONS

PS 3c A large number of important reactions involve the transfer of either electrons (oxidation/reduction reactions) or hydrogen ions (acid/base reactions) between reacting ions, molecules, or atoms. In other reactions, chemical bonds are broken by heat or light to form very reactive radicals with electrons ready to form new bonds. Radical reactions control many processes such as the presence of ozone and greenhouse gases in the atmosphere, burning and processing of fossil fuels, the formation of polymers, and explosions.

KEY
SE = Student Edition
ATE = Annotated Teacher Edition

Block 1 *(45 minutes)*

FOCUS *5 minutes*

❑ **Bellringer,** ATE (GENERAL). This activity has students make a list of the different types of reactions they have learned.

MOTIVATE *10 minutes*

❑ **Discussion,** ATE (GENERAL). Show students a browned wedge of apple, rusted piece of iron, and a burning candle and ask them to list evidence that a chemical reaction has occurred and how to stop those reactions from occurring.

TEACH *30 minutes*

❑ **Demonstration,** ATE (GENERAL). This demonstration illustrates three different oxidation rings of manganese corresponding to three oxidation states of manganese.

❑ **Skills Toolkit: Assigning Oxidation Numbers,** SE (GENERAL). Use this feature to walk students through assigning oxidation numbers.

❑ **Sample Problem A: Determining Oxidation Numbers,** SE (GENERAL). This problem demonstrates how to determine oxidation numbers.

HOMEWORK

❑ **Reading Skill Builder**, ATE (BASIC). Have students list things that they already know about electrochemistry.

❑ **Practice Sample Problems A,** SE (GENERAL). Determining Oxidation Numbers. Assign items 1a–1l.

❑ **Homework,** ATE (GENERAL). This assignment provides additional practice problems determining oxidation numbers like those in Practice Problem A.

OTHER RESOURCES

❑ **go.hrw.com**

❑ **www.scilinks.org**

Block 2 *(45 minutes)*
TEACH *35 minutes*

❑ **Demonstration,** ATE (GENERAL). This demonstration illustrates a simple redox reaction.

❑ **Skills Toolkit: Balancing Redox Equations Using the Half-Reaction Method,** SE (GENERAL). Use this feature to walk students through balancing redox reactions.

❑ **Sample Problem B: The Half-Reaction Method,** SE (GENERAL). This problem demonstrates how to balance redox equations using the half-reaction method.

❑ **Datasheet for In-text Lab: Redox Titration,** SE (GENERAL). Students determine the concentration of a solution using stoichiometry and volume data from a redox titration.

❑ **Datasheet for In-text Lab: Redox Titration—Mining Feasibility Study,** SE (GENERAL). Students determine the concentration of a solution using stoichiometry and volume data from a redox titration.

Lesson Plan *continued*

CLOSE *10 minutes*

- ❑ **Reteaching,** ATE (BASIC). Students work in pairs to write their own quiz questions and then trade quizzes with another pair of students.
- ❑ **Quiz,** ATE (GENERAL). This assignment has students answer questions about the concepts in this lesson.
- ❑ **Assessment Worksheet: Section Quiz** (GENERAL)

HOMEWORK

- ❑ **Practice Sample Problems B,** SE (GENERAL). The Half-Reaction Method. Assign items 1–4.
- ❑ **Homework,** ATE (GENERAL). This assignment provides additional practice problems using the half-reaction method like those in Practice Problem B.
- ❑ **Section Review,** SE (GENERAL). Assign items 1–12.
- ❑ **Skills Worksheet: Concept Review** (GENERAL)
- ❑ **Interactive Tutor for ChemFile,** Module 10: Electrochemistry, Topic: Electricity

OTHER RESOURCES

- ❑ **Group Activity**, ATE (BASIC). Group Activity is Basic Small groups of students research four naturally occurring redox reactions.
- ❑ **Teaching Tip,** ATE (ADVANCED). Show students how to use the half-reaction method in basic solutions. Skills Worksheet Sample Problem 2 will help to reinforce this skill.
- ❑ **Skills Worksheet: Problem Solving–The Half-Reaction Method, Sample Problem 1** (ADVANCED) This worksheet reinforces and extend the concepts and skills developed in Sample Problem B.
- ❑ **Skills Worksheet: Problem Solving–The Half-Reaction Method, Sample Problem 2** (ADVANCED) This worksheet reinforces balancing redox reactions using the half-reaction method in basic solutions.
- ❑ **go.hrw.com**
- ❑ **www.scilinks.org**

Lesson Plan

Section: Introduction to Electrochemistry

Pacing

Regular Schedule   with lab(s): N/A   without lab(s): 1 day
Block Schedule   with lab(s): N/A   without lab(s): ½ day

Objectives

1. Describe the relationship between voltage and the movement of electrons.

2. Identify the parts of an electrochemical cell and their functions.

3. Write electrode reactions for cathodes and anodes.

National Science Education Standards Covered

UNIFYING CONCEPTS AND PROCESSES

UCP 1 Systems, order, and organization

UCP 3 Change, constancy, and measurement

UCP 5 Form and function

PHYSICAL SCIENCE—CHEMICAL REACTIONS

PS 3a Chemical reactions occur all around us, for example in health care, cooking, cosmetics, and automobiles. Complex chemical reactions involving carbon-based molecules take place constantly in every cell in our bodies.

PS 3b Chemical reactions may release or consume energy. Some reactions such as the burning of fossil fuels release large amounts of energy by losing heat and by emitting light. Light can initiate many chemical reactions such as photosynthesis and the evolution of urban smog.

> **KEY**
> **SE** = Student Edition
> **ATE** = Annotated Teacher Edition

Block 3 *(45 minutes)*

FOCUS *5 minutes*

❑ **Bellringer** ATE (GENERAL). This activity has students write a brief paragraph about the requirements of an electric circuit.

MOTIVATE *10 minutes*

❑ **Activity,** ATE (BASIC). This activity has students examine a variety of batteries and determine whether oxidation or reduction occurs at the negative terminal of a battery.

TEACH *20 minutes*

❑ **Misconception Alert,** ATE (GENERAL). Use a battery and two 20 cm lengths of insulated wire to demonstrate that a complete circuit is needed to light a light bulb.

❑ **Reading Skill Builder**, ATE (BASIC). Have students use the headings and boldfaced terms to survey Section 2.

❑ **Using the Figure,** ATE (GENERAL). Use this feature to help students understand Figures 5 and 6.

❑ **Misconception Alert,** ATE (GENERAL). Point out that an anode can be the positive or the negative electrode. The anode is where oxidation occurs.

CLOSE *10 minutes*

❑ **Reteaching,** ATE (BASIC). Students work in small groups to make a table like the one provided in the ATE to organize information about anodic and cathodic processes.

❑ **Quiz,** ATE (GENERAL). This assignment has students answer questions about the concepts in this lesson.

❑ **Assessment Worksheet: Section Quiz** (GENERAL)

HOMEWORK

❑ **Skills Practice Worksheet: Concept Review** (GENERAL)

❑ **Section Review,** SE (GENERAL). Assign items 1–18.

❑ **Interactive Tutor for ChemFile,** Module 10: Electrochemistry, Topic: Electrochemical Cells

OTHER RESOURCES

❑ **go.hrw.com**

❑ **www.scilinks.org**

Lesson Plan

Section: Galvanic Cells

Pacing

Regular Schedule	**with lab(s):** $4\frac{1}{2}$ days	**without lab(s):** 3 days
Block Schedule	**with lab(s):** $2\frac{1}{2}$ days	**without lab(s):** $1\frac{1}{2}$ days

Objectives

1. Describe the operation of galvanic cells, including dry cells, lead-acid batteries, and fuel cells

2. Identify conditions that lead to corrosion and ways to prevent it.

3. Calculate cell voltage from a table of standard electrode potentials.

National Science Education Standards Covered

UNIFYING CONCEPTS AND PROCESSES

UCP 1 Systems, order, and organization

UCP 3 Change, constancy, and measurement

UCP 5 Form and function

PHYSICAL SCIENCE—CHEMICAL REACTIONS

PS 3a Chemical reactions occur all around us, for example in health care, cooking, cosmetics, and automobiles. Complex chemical reactions involving carbon-based molecules take place constantly in every cell in our bodies.

PS 3b Chemical reactions may release or consume energy. Some reactions such as the burning of fossil fuels release large amounts of energy by losing heat and by emitting light. Light can initiate many chemical reactions such as photosynthesis and the evolution of urban smog.

PS 3c A large number of important reactions involve the transfer of either electrons (oxidation/reduction reactions) or hydrogen ions (acid/base reactions) between reacting ions, molecules, or atoms. In other reactions, chemical bonds are broken by heat or light to form very reactive radicals with electrons ready to form new bonds. Radical reactions control many processes such as the presence of ozone and greenhouse gases in the atmosphere, burning and processing of fossil fuels, the formation of polymers, and explosions.

> **KEY**
> **SE** = Student Edition
> **ATE** = Annotated Teacher Edition

Block 4 *(45 minutes)*

FOCUS *5 minutes*

❑ **Bellringer** ATE (GENERAL). Students write a short paragraph about batteries and their usage.

MOTIVATE *15 minutes*

❑ **Activity**, ATE (BASIC). This activity has students model the electrochemical cell in Figure 8.

TEACH *20 minutes*

❑ **Transparency**, Galvanic Cell (GENERAL). This transparency illustrates the reaction in a galvanic cell. (Figure 8)

❑ **Using the Figure**, ATE (GENERAL). Use Figure 9 to help students compare two types of dry cells.

❑ **Transparency**, Dry Cells (GENERAL). This transparency shows that two kinds of dry cells use different electrolytes. (Figure 9)

❑ **Quick Lab: Listen Up**, SE (GENERAL). This lab has students pass current for a radio through a potato wedge. Students then answer two analysis questions about what they have done.

HOMEWORK

❑ **Reading Skill Builder**, ATE (BASIC). Have students use self-sticking notes to put a question mark next to passage in this section that they do not understand. Later, allow students class time to discuss their questions with a partner.

❑ **Inclusion Strategy**, ATE (BASIC). Have developmentally delayed students make a collage of different items that require batteries to operate or draw a diagram of a battery and label the negative and positive terminals.

OTHER RESOURCES

❑ **go.hrw.com**

❑ **www.scilinks.org**

Block 5 *(45 minutes)*

TEACH *45 minutes*

❑ **Demonstration,** ATE (GENERAL). This demonstration illustrates how to make a six-cell battery using lemons.

❑ **Transparency,** Fuel Cell (GENERAL). This transparency illustrates the reactions in a fuel cell. (Figure 11)

❑ **Transparency,** Corrosion Cell (GENERAL). This transparency illustrates the reactions in a corrosion cell. (Figure 12)

HOMEWORK

❑ **Science and Technology,** SE (GENERAL). Have students read this feature about fuel cells and answer the two questions that follow.

OTHER RESOURCES

❑ **Biology Connection,** ATE (ADVANCED). Have students study the types of bacteria that contribute to corrosion problems.

❑ **Demonstration,** ATE (GENERAL). This demonstration allows students to predict the outcome of two reactions.

❑ **go.hrw.com**

❑ **www.scilinks.org**

Block 6 *(45 minutes)*

TEACH *30 minutes*

❑ **Activity,** ATE (GENERAL). Use a voltmeter to measure the voltage of several batteries with different voltage ratings.

❑ **Sample Problem C: Calculating Cell Voltage,** SE (GENERAL). This problem demonstrates how to calculate cell voltage.

❑ **CBL Probeware Lab: Micro-Voltaic Cells,** (ADVANCED). Chapter Resource File. In this lab, students will use a calculator-interfaced voltage probe to measure potential differences between various pairs of half cells.

CLOSE *15 minutes*

❑ **Reteaching,** ATE (BASIC). Students create a concept map using the key terms from this section.

❑ **Quiz,** ATE (GENERAL). This assignment has students answer questions about the concepts in this lesson.

❑ **Assessment Worksheet: Section Quiz** (GENERAL)

HOMEWORK

❑ **Skills Worksheet: Concept Review** (GENERAL). This worksheet reviews the main concepts and problem-solving skills of this section.

❑ **Practice Sample Problems C,** SE (GENERAL). Calculating Cell Voltage. Assign items 1–3.

❑ **Homework,** ATE (BASIC). This assignment has students calculate cell voltages. (Practice Problem C)

❑ **Section Review,** SE (GENERAL). Assign items 1–8.

OTHER RESOURCES

❑ **Using the Table,** ATE (ADVANCED). Refer students to the activity series shown in Appendix A and ask them to compare its arrangement with that of Table 1.

❑ **Skills Worksheet: Problem Solving–Electrochemistry, Sample Problems 1 and 2** (ADVANCED) These worksheets reinforce and extend the concepts and skills developed in Sample Problem C.

❑ **go.hrw.com**

❑ **www.scilinks.org**

Lesson Plan

Section: Electrolytic Cells

Pacing

Regular Schedule   **with lab(s):** 3 days   **without lab(s):** 2 days
Block Schedule   **with lab(s):** 1½ days   **without lab(s):** 1 day

Objectives

1. Describe how electrolytic cells work.

2. Describe the process of electrolysis in the decomposition of water and the production of metals.

3. Describe the process of electroplating.

National Science Education Standards Covered
UNIFYING CONCEPTS AND PROCESSES

UCP 1 Systems, order, and organization

UCP 2 Evidence, models, and explanation

UCP 5 Form and function

PHYSICAL SCIENCE—CHEMICAL REACTIONS

PS 3a Chemical reactions occur all around us, for example in health care, cooking, cosmetics, and automobiles. Complex chemical reactions involving carbon-based molecules take place constantly in every cell in our bodies.

PS 3b Chemical reactions may release or consume energy. Some reactions such as the burning of fossil fuels release large amounts of energy by losing heat and by emitting light. Light can initiate many chemical reactions such as photosynthesis and the evolution of urban smog.

PS 3c A large number of important reactions involve the transfer of either electrons (oxidation/reduction reactions) or hydrogen ions (acid/base reactions) between reacting ions, molecules, or atoms. In other reactions, chemical bonds are broken by heat or light to form very reactive radicals with electrons ready to form new bonds. Radical reactions control many processes such as the presence of ozone and greenhouse gases in the atmosphere, burning and processing of fossil fuels, the formation of polymers, and explosions.

> **KEY**
> **SE** = Student Edition
> **ATE** = Annotated Teacher Edition

Block 7 *(45 minutes)*

FOCUS *5 minutes*

❑ **Bellringer** ATE (GENERAL). Students review what they have learned about electrochemical cells with a partner.

MOTIVATE *10 minutes*

❑ **Discussion,** ATE (BASIC). Use Figure 15 and the list of questions provided under this heading in the ATE to have students analyze the figure.

TEACH *30 minutes*

❑ **Transparency,** Refining Copper Using an Electrolytic Cell. (GENERAL) This transparency illustrates the industrial mining of copper. (Figure 15)

❑ **Demonstration,** ATE (GENERAL). This demonstration illustrates the electrolysis of KI.

❑ **Transparency,** Downs Cell (GENERAL). This transparency illustrates how the electrolysis of molten NaCl forms the elements sodium and chlorine in a Downs cell. (Figure 17)

HOMEWORK

❑ **Homework,** ATE (BASIC). This assignment has students make a list of electroplated objects in their home and identify the metals involved in the plating.

OTHER RESOURCES

❑ **Using the Figure,** ATE (ADVANCED). Ask students to determine the overall reaction and use the equation to determine which test tube in Figure 16 is filling with oxygen and which is filling with hydrogen.

❑ **Skill Builder,** ATE (ADVANCED). Have students research the electroless plating process.

❑ **go.hrw.com**

❑ **www.scilinks.org**

| Lesson Plan *continued*

Block 8 *(45 minutes)*

TEACH *30 minutes*

❏ **Transparency,** Hall-Héroult Process (GENERAL). This transparency illustrates how the Hall-Héroult process is used to make aluminum by the electrolysis of dissolved alumina. (Figure 18)

❏ **Transparency,** Electroplating (GENERAL). This transparency illustrates the process of electroplating. (Figure 19)

❏ **Observation Lab: Electroplating for Corrosion Protection,** (GENERAL) Students construct and use an electrolytic cell to plate one metal onto another. They then test the plated metal to determine how well it resists corrosion by an acidic solution.

CLOSE *15 minutes*

❏ **Assessment Worksheet: Section Quiz** (GENERAL)

❏ **Reteaching,** ATE (BASIC). Students outline the main ideas of the section.

❏ **Quiz,** ATE (GENERAL). This assignment has students answer questions about the concepts in this lesson.

HOMEWORK

❏ **Skills Worksheet: Concept Review** (GENERAL) This worksheet reviews the main concepts and problem-solving skills of this section.

❏ **Section Review,** SE (GENERAL). Assign items 1–15.

OTHER RESOURCES

❏ **Group Activity,** ATE (ADVANCED). Have students research and do a visual presentation on the uses of aluminum and how those uses relate to aluminum's chemical and physical properties.

❏ **Focus on Graphing,** SE

❏ **go.hrw.com**

❏ **www.scilinks.org**

END OF CHAPTER REVIEW AND ASSESSMENT RESOURCES

❏ **Mixed Review,** SE (GENERAL).

❏ **Alternate Assessment,** SE (GENERAL).

❏ **Technology and Learning,** SE (GENERAL).

❏ **Standardized Test Prep,** SE (GENERAL).

❏ **Assessment Worksheet: Chapter Test** (GENERAL)

❏ **Test Item Listing for ExamView® Test Generator**

Name _____ Class _____ Date _____

Quick Lab

Listen Up

OBJECTIVE

Create a simple galvanic cell.

MATERIALS

For each group of 2–4 students:

- alligator clips (2)
- copper strip
- earphone
- raw potato
- zinc strip

Always wear safety goggles and a lab apron to protect your eyes and clothing. If you get a chemical in your eyes, immediately flush the chemical out at the eyewash station while calling to your teacher. Know the location of the emergency lab shower and eyewash station and the procedures for using them.

Procedure

1. Press a zinc strip and a copper strip into a raw potato. The strips should be about 0.5 cm apart but should not touch one another.

2. While listening to the earphone, touch one wire from the earphone to one of the metal strips and the other wire from the earphone to the second metal strip using alligator clips. Record your observations.

3. While listening to the earphone, touch both wires to a single metal strip. Record your observations.

Analysis

1. Compare your results from step 2 with your results from step 3. Suggest an explanation for any similarities or differences.

   When the wires from the earphone are touched to both strips, the earphone

   makes a crackling noise. Touching the wires to only one strip produces no

   sound. A complete circuit exists only when the wires are connected to sepa-

   rate strips.

2. Suggest an explanation for the sound.

   The potato "battery" is producing an electric current in the earphone, caus-

   ing it to produce a crackling sound.

DATASHEETS FOR IN-TEXT LAB

Redox Titration: Mining Feasibility Study

Teacher Notes

MATERIALS

- beaker, 400 mL
- beakers, 250 mL (2)
- burets (2)
- distilled water
- double buret clamp
- Erlenmeyer flasks, 125 mL (4)

- graduated cylinder, 100 mL
- H_2SO_4, 1.0 M
- $KMnO_4$, 0.0200 M
- ring stand
- unknown solution, (0.25 M $FeSO_4$)
- wash bottle

ANSWERS

Procedure

Prepare the burets for the titration using $KMnO_4$ solution in one buret and $FeSO_4$ solution in the other. Put a drop of $KMnO_4$ solution in one Erlenmeyer flask to serve as a color standard to recognize the end point.

Put 10.0 mL of the $FeSO_4$ solution in an Erlenmeyer flask. Add 5 mL of 1.0 M H_2SO_4. Slowly add $KMnO_4$ solution from the buret. Swirl after each drop is added. When the color matches the standard, record the final volumes of the burets. Repeat the titration procedure twice.

Sample Data

Trial	Initial FeSO₄ volume (mL)	Final FeSO₄ volume (mL)	Initial KMnO₄ volume (mL)	Final KMnO₄ volume (mL)
1	50.0	40.0	50.0	25.0
2	40.0	30.0	50.0	25.2
3	30.0	20.0	50.0	24.8

Calculations

Redox equation: $MnO_4^- + 8H^+ + 5Fe^{2+} \rightarrow Mn^{2+} + 5Fe^{3+} + 4H_2O$

Moles and grams of $FeSO_4$ in 10 mL of sample

$(0.025 \text{ L} \times 0.02 \text{ M } MnO_4^-) \times (5Fe^{2+}/ MnO_4^-) = 0.0025$ moles Fe^{2+} in 10ml
0.0025 moles $\times$ 152 g/mole = 0.38 g $FeSO_4$/10 ml

Moles, grams, and percentage of iron(II) in 10 mL of the sample:

0.0025 moles iron(II)/10 ml $\times$ 56 g/mole = 0.14g iron (II)/10 ml

0.14 g/10 g $\times$ 100% = 1.4% iron(II)

Number of kilograms of iron that the company could extract from the mine each year, assuming that 1.0×10^5 L of slurry could be mined per day:

(0.14 g/10 ml) = 0.14 kg/L

0.14 kg/L $\times$ 1.0 $\times$ 10^5 L/day $\times$ 365 days/year = 5 110 000 kg/yr

Skills Practice Lab

Redox Titration

You are a chemist working for a chemical analysis firm. A large pharmaceutical company has hired you to help salvage some products that were damaged by a small fire in their warehouse. Although there was only minimal smoke and fire damage to the warehouse and products, the sprinkler system ruined the labeling on many of the pharmaceuticals. The firm's best-selling products are iron tonics used to treat low-level anemia. The tonics are produced from hydrated iron(II) sulfate, $FeSO_4 \cdot 7H_2O$. The different types of tonics contain different concentrations of $FeSO_4$. You have been hired to help the pharmaceutical company figure out the proper label for each bottle of tonic.

In the chapter "Acids and Bases" you studied acid-base titrations in which an unknown amount of acid is titrated with a carefully measured amount of base. In this procedure a similar approach called a redox titration is used. In a redox titration, the reducing agent, Fe^{2+}, is oxidized to Fe^{3+} by the oxidizing agent, MnO_4^-. When this process occurs, the Mn in MnO_4^- changes from a +7 to a +2 oxidation state and has a noticeably different color. You can use this color change in the same way that you used the color change of phenolphthalein in acid-base titrations—to signify a redox reaction end point. When the reaction is complete, any excess MnO_4^- added to the reaction mixture will give the solution a pink or purple color. The volume data from the titration, the known molarity of the $KMnO_4$ solution, and the mole ratio from the following balanced redox equation will give you the information you need to calculate the molarity of the $FeSO_4$ solution.

$$5Fe^{2+}(aq) + MnO_4^-(aq) + 8H^+(aq) \rightarrow 5Fe^{3+}(aq) + Mn^{2+}(aq) + 4H_2O(l)$$

To determine how to label the bottles, you must determine the concentration of iron(II) ions in the sample from an unlabeled bottle from the warehouse by answering the following questions:

- How can the volume data obtained from the titration and the mole ratios from the balanced redox reaction be used to determine the concentration of the sample?

- Which tonic is in the sample, given information about the concentration of each tonic?

OBJECTIVES

Demonstrate proficiency in performing redox titrations and recognizing the end point of a redox reaction.

Determine the concentration of a solution using stoichiometry and volume data from a titration.

Redox Titration *continued*

MATERIALS

- beaker, 250 mL (2)
- beaker, 400 mL
- burets (2)
- distilled water
- double buret clamp
- Erlenmeyer flask, 125 mL (4)
- $FeSO_4$ solution
- graduated cylinder, 100 mL
- H_2SO_4, 1.0 M
- $KMnO_4$, 0.0200 M
- ring stand
- wash bottle

 Always wear safety goggles, gloves, and a lab apron to protect your eyes and clothing. If you get a chemical in your eyes, immediately flush the chemical out at the eyewash station while calling to your teacher. Know the location of the emergency lab shower and eyewash station and the procedures for using them.

 Do not touch any chemicals. If you get a chemical on your skin or clothing, wash the chemical off at the sink while calling to your teacher. Make sure you carefully read the labels and follow the precautions on all containers of chemicals that you use. If there are no precautions stated on the label, ask your teacher what precautions to follow. Do not taste any chemicals or items used in the laboratory. Never return leftovers to their original container; take only small amounts to avoid wasting supplies.

Call your teacher in the event of a spill. Spills should be cleaned up promptly, according to your teacher's directions.

Acids and bases are corrosive. If an acid or base spills onto your skin or clothing, wash the area immediately with running water. Call your teacher in the event of an acid spill. Acid or base spills should be cleaned up promptly.

Never put broken glass in a regular waste container. Broken glass should be disposed of separately according to your teacher's instructions.

Procedure

1. Put on safety goggles, gloves, and a lab apron.

2. Clean two 50 mL burets with a buret brush and distilled water. Rinse each buret at least three times with distilled water to remove any contaminants.

3. Label two 250 mL beakers "0.0200 M $KMnO_4$," and "$FeSO_4$ solution." Label three of the flasks 1, 2, and 3. Label the 400 mL beaker "Waste." Label one buret "$KMnO_4$" and the other "$FeSO_4$."

4. Measure approximately 75 mL of 0.0200 M $KMnO_4$, and pour it into the appropriately labeled beaker. Obtain approximately 75 mL of $FeSO_4$ solution, and pour it into the appropriately labeled beaker.

5. Rinse one buret three times with a few milliliters of 0.0200 M $KMnO_4$ from the appropriately labeled beaker. Collect these rinses in the waste beaker. Rinse the other buret three times with small amounts of $FeSO_4$ solution from the appropriately labeled beaker. Collect these rinses in the waste beaker.

6. Set up the burets. Fill one buret with approximately 50 mL of the 0.0200 M $KMnO_4$ from the beaker, and fill the other buret with approximately 50 mL of the $FeSO_4$ solution from the other beaker.

7. With the waste beaker underneath its tip, open the $KMnO_4$ buret long enough to be sure the buret tip is filled. Repeat for the $FeSO_4$ buret.

8. Add 50 mL of distilled water to one of the 125 mL Erlenmeyer flasks, and add one drop of 0.0200 M $KMnO_4$ to the flask. Set this aside to use as a color standard to compare with the titration and to determine the end point.

9. Record the initial buret readings for both solutions in your data table. Add 10.0 mL of the hydrated iron(II) sulfate, $FeSO_4 \cdot 7H_2O$, solution to flask 1. Add 5 mL of 1.0 M H_2SO_4 to the $FeSO_4$ solution in this flask. The acid will help keep the Fe^{2+} ions in the reduced state, allowing you time to titrate.

10. Slowly add $KMnO_4$ from the buret to the $FeSO_4$ in the flask while swirling the flask. When the color of the solution matches the color standard you prepared in step **8,** record the final readings of the burets in your data table.

11. Empty the titration flask into the waste beaker. Repeat the titration procedure in steps **9** and **10** with flasks 2 and 3.

12. Always clean up the lab and all equipment after use. Dispose of the contents of the waste beaker in the container designated by your teacher. Also pour the contents of the color-standard flask into this container. Wash your hands thoroughly after cleaning up the area and equipment.

| Redox Titration *continued*

TABLE 1 TITRATION DATA

Trial	Initial KmnO$_4$ volume	Final KMnO$_4$ volume	Initial FeSO$_4$ volume	Final FeSO$_4$ volume
1	50.0	35.0	50.0	40.0
2	35.0	20.5	40.0	30.0
3	20.5	5.0	30.0	20.0

Analysis

1. Analyzing Data Calculate the number of moles of MnO$_4^-$ reduced in each trial.

Trial 1: 15.0 mL KMnO$_4$ × 1 L/1000 mL × 0.020 mol KMnO$_4$/1L =

3.0 × 10^{-4} mol KMnO$_4$

Trial 2: 14.5 mL KMnO$_4$ × 1 L/1000 mL × 0.020 mol KMnO$_4$/1L =

2.9 × 10^{-4} mol KMnO$_4$

Trial 3: 15.5 mL KMnO$_4$ × 1 L/1000 mL × 0.020 mol KMnO$_4$/1L =

3.1 × 10^{-4} mol KMnO$_4$

2. Analyzing Data Calculate the number of moles of Fe^{2+} oxidized in each trial.

The ratio of Fe^{2+} to MnO$_4^-$ is 5:1

Trial 1: 3.0 × 10^{-4} mol MnO$_4^-$ × 5 mol Fe^{2+}/1 mol MnO$_4^-$ =

1.5 × 10^{-3} mol Fe^{2+}

Trial 2: 2.9 × 10^{-4} mol MnO$_4^-$ × 5 mol Fe^{2+}/1 mol MnO$_4^-$ =

1.5 × 10^{-3} mol Fe^{2+}

Trial 3: 3.1 × 10^{-4} mol MnO$_4^-$ × 5 mol Fe^{2+}/1 mol MnO$_4^-$ =

1.6 × 10^{-3} mol Fe^{2+}

3. Analyzing Data Calculate the average concentration (molarity) of the iron tonic.

average molarity = 1.5 × 10^{-3} mol Fe^{2+}/10.0 mL × 1000 mL/1 L =
0.15 M Fe^{2+}

Name _____ Class _____ Date _____

Redox Titration *continued*

4. **Explaining Events** Explain why it was important to rinse the burets with $KMnO_4$ or $FeSO_4$ before adding the solutions. (Hint: Consider what would happen to the concentration of each solution if it were added to a buret that had been rinsed only with distilled water.)

The concentrations of each solution is very important. If you rinse the buret

only with distilled water, the solutions might be diluted if there was any

water left in the buret. By using the solution being measured to rinse the

buret, you can be sure any solution left behind will not dilute the solution

added.

Conclusions

5. **Evaluating Data** The company makes three different types of iron tonics: Feravide A, with a concentration of 0.145 M $FeSO_4$; Feravide Extra-Strength, with 0.225 M $FeSO_4$; and Feravide Jr., with 0.120 M $FeSO_4$. Which tonic is your sample?

The sample tonic is most likely Feravide A, 0.145 M $FeSO_4$.

6. **Evaluating Methods** What possible sources of error can you identify with this procedure? If you can think of ways to eliminate them, ask your teacher to approve your plan, and run the procedure again.

Suggestions for improving the procedure will vary. Possible suggestions

include performing repeated trials or using larger volumes for the titration.

Be sure answers include safe, carefully planned procedures.

Name _____ Class _____ Date _____

Redox Titration *continued*

Extensions

1. Research and Communication Blueprints are based on a photochemical reaction. The paper is treated with a solution of iron(III) ammonium citrate and potassium hexacyanoferrate(III) and dried in the dark. When a tracing-paper drawing is placed on the blueprint paper and exposed to light, Fe^{3+} ions are reduced to Fe^{2+} ions, which react with hexacyanoferrate(III) ions in the moist paper to form the blue color on the paper. The lines of the drawing block the light and prevent the reduction of Fe^{3+} ions, resulting in white lines. Find out how sepia prints are made, and report on this information.

Sepia printing is similar to blue-print printing. In sepia printing, the

potassium hexacyanoferrate(III) oxidizes the crystals of silver in the print

so that they become silver ions again. Then the print is redeveloped in

sodium sulfide.

2. Building Models Electrochemical cells are based on the process of electron flow in a system with varying potential differences. Batteries are composed of such systems and contain different chemicals for different purposes and price ranges. You can make simple experimental batteries using metal wires and items such as lemons, apples, and potatoes. What are some other "home-made" battery sources, and what is the role of these food items in producing electrical energy that can be measured as battery power? Explain your answers.

Answers will vary. The food is the conductor that completes the circuit

between the two metals, each of which has a different reduction potential. In

terms of a traditional cell, the food acts as both the porous barrier that

separates the metal and the solution of aqueous ions that completes the

circuit.

OBSERVATION

Electroplating for Corrosion Protection

Teacher Notes

TIME REQUIRED One 45-minute lab period with drying oven; two 45-minute lab periods otherwise

SKILLS ACQUIRED
Collecting data
Communicating
Identifying patterns
Inferring
Interpreting
Organizing and analyzing data

RATING   Easy ← 1   2   3   4 → Hard
Teacher Prep–3
Student Set-Up–3
Concept Level–2
Clean Up–2

THE SCIENTIFIC METHOD

Make Observations Students will observe and compare the results of electro-plating copper wire with iron and with zinc.

Analyze the Results Analysis question 2 and Conclusions questions 3 and 4

Draw Conclusions Conclusions questions 3 and 4.

Communicate the Results Analysis question 2 and Conclusions questions 3 and 4

MATERIALS

To prepare 1.00 L of the $FeCl_3$ plating solution, observe the required precautions. Dissolve 40.0 g $FeCl_3 \cdot 6H_2O$ in 900 mL of distilled water and 50 mL of ethanol. Add more water to dilute to 1.00 L.

To prepare 1.00 L of the $ZnSO_4$ plating solution, dissolve 50.0 g $ZnSO_4 \cdot 7H_2O$, 24.0 g NH_4Cl, and 40.0 g ammonium citrate, $(NH_4)_2HC_6H_5O_7$, in 900 mL of distilled water. Add more water to dilute to 1.00 L.

To prepare 1.00 L of 1.00 M HCl, observe the required precautions. Add 82.6 mL of concentrated HCl to enough distilled water to make 1.00 L of solution. Add the acid slowly, and stop frequently to stir it in order to avoid overheating.

Any size of copper wire will do. The procedure that generated the sample data was performed with soft, bare, 18 gauge wire.

Use a 6 V "lantern battery" or its equivalent. DO NOT use a high-amperage 6 V battery such as those designed for supplying current for the spark in gasoline-powered motors.

Although optional, the use of the drying oven is strongly recommended. Otherwise, if the lab is to be performed quantitatively, the wires must dry overnight after plating and again after testing them in 1.0 M HCl.

Electroplating for Corrosion Protection *continued*

SAFETY CAUTIONS

Remind students that objects from the drying oven will be very hot. They should use beaker tongs or a hot mitt to pick them up.

Students should not handle concentrated acid or base solutions.

Wear safety goggles, a face shield, impermeable gloves, and a lab apron when preparing the HCl. Work in a hood known to be in operating condition, with another person present nearby to call for help in case of an emergency. Be sure you are within 30 s walk of a properly working safety shower and eyewash station.

In case of an acid or base spill, first dilute with water. Then mop up the spill with wet cloths or a wet cloth mop while wearing disposable plastic gloves. Designate separate cloths or mops for acid and base spills.

Observe the precautions on the ethanol bottle's label when preparing the $FeCl_3$ solution.

Remind students of the following safety precautions:

- Always wear safety goggles, gloves, and a lab apron to protect your eyes and clothing. If you get a chemical in your eyes, immediately flush the chemical out at the eyewash station while calling to your teacher. Know the location of the emergency lab shower and the eyewash station and the procedure for using them.

- Do not touch any chemicals. If you get a chemical on your skin or clothing, wash the chemical off at the sink while calling to your teacher. Make sure you carefully read the labels and follow the precautions on all containers of chemicals that you use. If there are no precautions stated on the label, ask your teacher what precautions you should follow. Do not taste any chemicals or items used in the laboratory. Never return leftovers to their original containers; take only small amounts to avoid wasting supplies.

- Call your teacher in the event of a spill. Spills should be cleaned up promptly, according to your teacher's directions.

- Never put broken glass in a regular waste container. Broken glass should be disposed of properly.

DISPOSAL

Set out six disposal containers: three bins and three bottles, or other similar containers. Of the three bins, use one for copper wires, one for zinc metal strips, and one for iron metal strips. Of the three containers, use one for the $FeCl_3$ solution, one for the $ZnSO_4$ solution, and one for the contents of the *Waste* beaker and the HCl from the test tubes.

The metal strips should be cleaned with soap and water, rinsed, and dried for reuse the next time students perform this lab. The copper wires can also be reused after they have been treated with 1.0 M HCl and all of the zinc or iron has been removed. The iron and zinc solutions should be saved and reused.

Pour the HCl that has been used in treating the copper wires into the disposal container for the *Waste* beaker. Add 1.0 M NaOH to the mixture in the *Waste* beaker container to precipitate the iron and zinc as hydroxides. Filter the mixture, placing the precipitate in the trash. Then neutralize the filtrate with 1.0 M H_3PO_4 until the pH is between 5 and 9, and pour it down the drain.

TECHNIQUES TO DEMONSTRATE

Be sure to show students the proper order for the connections between the electrodes and the battery, reminding them to check that they have connected the appropriate metal to the battery's positive electrode. Point out the importance of performing the steps in exactly the same manner for the different wire treatments. Each wire should be plated for the same amount of time, at the same depth in the beaker, and with similar amounts of plating solution. Similarly, the testing steps should be performed with the same amounts of acid for the same amount of time.

TIPS AND TRICKS

Discuss reduction and oxidation. Make sure students realize that a different reaction is occurring at each electrode. Many will recognize that plating (reduction) is occurring at one electrode but will not understand that oxidation of the metal is occurring at the other.

Name _____ Class _____ Date _____

Skills Practice Lab

Electroplating for Corrosion Protection

SITUATION

Your company has been contacted by a manufacturer of electrical circuits. The company uses 1.0 M HCl to clean newly manufactured circuits. They've decided to store the acid in large metal tanks instead of reagent bottles. The company has narrowed down the choices to copper, zinc-plated copper, and iron-plated copper. You have been asked to evaluate these choices.

BACKGROUND

Solutions of acids can oxidize some metals. The displacement reaction of magnesium and hydrochloric acid is an example.

$$\underset{0}{Mg(s)} + \underset{+1-1}{2HCl(aq)} \longrightarrow \underset{+2\ -1}{MgCl_2(aq)} + \underset{0}{H_2(g)}$$

Metals that react can be electroplated with a thin layer of a less reactive metal. In an electroplating cell, electrical energy is used to reduce metal ions in solution, causing it to adhere to the surface of an object functioning as an anode. **Figure 1** shown here summarizes the apparatus and the process.

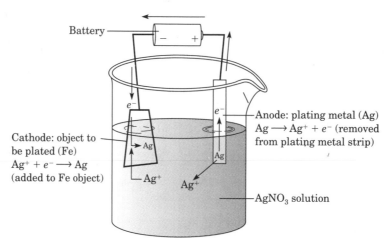

Figure 1

PROBLEM

You must first prepare samples of the plated metals. Then you must test each one in 1.0 M HCl to determine which resists corrosion the best.

OBJECTIVES

Construct an electrolytic cell with an electrolyte, two electrodes, and a battery.

Use the electrolytic cell to plate one metal onto another.

Test the plated metals and a sample of the original metal to determine how well they resist corrosion by an acidic solution.

Relate the results to the activity series and to standard reduction potentials.

Name _____ Class _____ Date _____

Electroplating for Corrosion Protection *continued*

MATERIALS

- balance
- battery, 6 V (lantern type)
- beaker, 400 mL
- beakers, 150 mL (3)
- copper wire, 10 cm lengths (3)
- distilled water
- $FeCl_3$ plating solution
- gloves
- HCl, 1.0 M
- iron strip, 1 cm $\times$ 8 cm
- lab apron
- safety goggles
- steel wool

- stick-on label
- stopwatch or clock with second hand
- test-tube rack
- test tubes, large (3)
- wax pencil
- wire with alligator clips (2 pieces)
- zinc strip, 1 cm $\times$ 8 cm
- $ZnSO_4$ plating solution

Optional equipment

- beaker tongs
- drying oven

Always wear safety goggles, gloves, and a lab apron to protect your eyes and clothing. If you get a chemical in your eyes, immediately flush the chemical out at the eyewash station while calling to your teacher. Know the location of the emergency lab shower and eyewash station and the procedures for using them.

Do not touch any chemicals. If you get a chemical on your skin or clothing, wash the chemical off at the sink while calling to your teacher. Make sure you carefully read the labels and follow the precautions on all containers of chemicals that you use. If there are no precautions stated on the label, ask your teacher what precautions to follow. Do not taste any chemicals or items used in the laboratory. Never return leftovers to their original container; take only small amounts to avoid wasting supplies.

Call your teacher in the event of a spill. Spills should be cleaned up promptly, according to your teacher's directions.

Acids and bases are corrosive. If an acid or base spills onto your skin or clothing, wash the area immediately with running water. Call your teacher in the event of an acid spill. Acid or base spills should be cleaned up promptly.

Do not heat glassware that is broken, chipped, or cracked. Use tongs or a hot mitt to handle heated glassware and other equipment because hot glassware does not always look hot.

Name _____ Class _____ Date _____

Electroplating for Corrosion Protection *continued*

PART 1–PREPARATION

1. Put on safety goggles, gloves, and a lab apron.

2. Label two of the 150 mL beakers *FeCl₃* and *ZnSO₄*. Label the 400 mL beaker *Waste*.

3. Make loops on one end of each of the wires. Using a piece of a stick-on label, label the wires *Cu*, *Fe/Cu*, and *Zn/Cu* just below the loops.

4. Polish each wire and metal strip with steel wool.

5. Using the laboratory balance, measure the mass of the *Fe/Cu* wire. Record it in your data table.

PART 2–PLATING

6. Attach one end of a wire with alligator clips to the loop on the *Fe/Cu* wire. Attach the alligator clip on the other end of the wire to the negative ($-$) terminal of the battery.

7. Attach one end of the other wire with alligator clips to the iron strip. Clip the other end of this wire to the positive ($+$) terminal of the battery, as shown in **Figure 2** below. Keep the iron strip away from the copper wire.

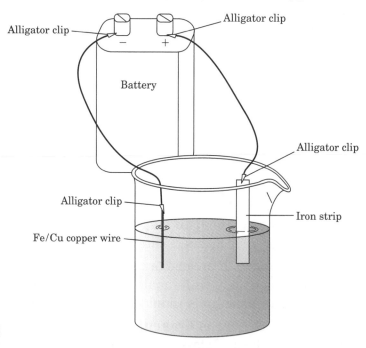

Figure 2

8. Pour 80 mL of the FeCl₃ solution into the *FeCl₃* beaker.

9. Using a stopwatch or clock with second hand to measure the time, immerse both the copper wire and the iron strip in the beaker, being careful to keep the alligator clips out of the solution. Use the loop to hang the wire on the beaker.

10. After about 5 min, remove the copper wire and the iron strip. Record the time elapsed to the nearest 1.0 s.

Electroplating for Corrosion Protection *continued*

11. Rinse the *Fe/Cu* wire with distilled water, collecting the rinse water in the *Waste* beaker. Record your observations about the *Fe/Cu* wire in your data table.

12. Hold the unplated *Zn/Cu* wire close to the plated *Fe/Cu* wire. Use a wax pencil to make a mark on the *Zn/Cu* and *Cu* wires at about the same level as the edge of the plating on the *Fe/Cu* wire. Measure and record the masses of these wires.

13. Repeat steps **6–11** with the zinc metal strip, zinc sulfate solution in the *ZnSO₄* beaker, and the wire labeled *Zn/Cu*. Be certain to plate the wire for exactly the same amount of time. Also be certain that the *Zn/Cu* wire is immersed up to the wax pencil mark.

14. Place the plated wires in the unlabeled 150 mL beaker so that they are not touching each other. Either allow the wires to dry in the beaker overnight, or place the beaker in a drying oven for 10 min. **Remember to use beaker tongs to handle all glassware that has been in the drying oven.**

15. After the wires have cooled, measure and record the masses of the *Fe/Cu* wire and the *Zn/Cu* wire in the data table.

16. In your data table rewrite the original mass of the *Cu* wire in the *New mass of wire (g)* row under the *Cu* column.

PART 3–TESTING REACTIVITY

17. Fill each of the test tubes about one-third full of 1.0 M HCl. Place the test tubes in a test-tube rack.

18. Place one of the wires into each of the test tubes so that only the plated parts are in the HCl solution. Wait about 5 min.

19. Remove the wires, and rinse them with distilled water, collecting the rinse in the *Waste* beaker. Record the time and your observations about the wires in your data table. Place the wires in the unlabeled 150 mL beaker so that they do not touch. Dry the wires overnight, or place them in a drying oven for 10 min.

20. Remove the beaker of wires from the drying oven and allow it to cool. **Remember to use beaker tongs to handle beakers that have been in the drying oven.**

21. Measure and record the masses of the wires in your data table as *Mass of wire after HCl (g)*.

22. Your teacher will provide separate disposal containers for each solution, each metal, and contents of the *Waste* beaker. The HCl from the test tubes can be poured into the same container as the contents of the *Waste* beaker.

Name _____ Class _____ Date _____

| **Electroplating for Corrosion Protection** *continued*

TABLE 1: ELECTROPLATING DATA

	Cu	Fe/Cu	Zn/Cu
Mass of wire (g)	0.77	0.77	0.77
Plating time (s)	n/a	301.00	299.00
New mass of wire (g)	0.77	0.82	0.89
HCl time (s)	300.00	300.00	300.00
Mass of wire after HCl (g)	0.77	0.77	0.77

Observations

Students' data should also include observations about the wire. After

plating, the metals should be visible on the wire. The iron will look dark and

silvery, and the zinc will look silvery, but lighter than the iron. After

treatment with HCl, little of the plated metals will remain.

Analysis

1. **Applying Models** Write the equation for the half-reactions occurring on the metal strip and the copper wire in the $FeCl_3$ and $ZnSO_4$ beakers. Which is the anode in each one? Which is the cathode in each one?

   iron strip: $Fe(s) \longrightarrow Fe^{3+}(aq) + 3e^-$, anode

   copper wire: $Fe^{3+}(aq) + 3e^- \longrightarrow Fe(s)$, cathode

   zinc strip: $Zn(s) \longrightarrow Zn^{2+}(aq) + 2e^-$, anode

   copper wire: $Zn^{2+}(aq) + 2e^- \longrightarrow Zn(s)$, cathode

2. **Analyzing Data** How many grams and moles of iron and zinc were plated onto the *Fe/Cu* and *Zn/Cu* wires?
   0.05 g Fe, 0.12 g Zn
   9×10^{-4} mol Fe, 1.8×10^{-3} mol Zn

Conclusions

3. **Analyzing Results** Which metal or metal combination was the least reactive in HCl? Explain the basis for your conclusion.

   The untreated copper wire was least reactive. When the zinc- and iron-plated

   wires were placed in the HCl, bubbling occurred, indicating a reaction.

Electroplating for Corrosion Protection *continued*

4. Evaluating Conclusions What disadvantages relating to the use of the least reactive metal for the tanks can you think of?

Students' suggestions about the disadvantages of copper will vary. Possible

answers include the following: copper is soft and malleable, so the tanks

might be easily harmed; copper costs more than iron or zinc.

_____

Extensions

1. Research and Communication Find out what measures are taken to try to prevent metal bridges and buildings from corroding, and prepare a chart to show the different methods, their relative costs, and their general uses.

Students will find a variety of methods in use. The Teflon used in the Statue

of Liberty prevents the iron and copper in the statue from coming into direct

contact. In this way, the redox reactions that led to the crumbling and corro-

sion of the previous iron framework can be greatly reduced. Other coatings

and paints work the same way to keep the reactants separated. In other

approaches, a sacrificial anode, which is made of a more active metal than

the main part of the item, is used. This approach is used on some ships'

hulls. Another possibility is to apply a small amount of voltage to an object

so that reduction rather than oxidation is favored.

Skills Practice Lab

Micro-Voltaic Cells

Time Required

One lab period

Skills Acquired

- Collecting data
- Experimenting
- Organizing and analyzing data
- Interpreting
- Identifying/recognizing patterns

The Scientific Method

- **Make Observations** Students will measure potential differences between half-cell pairs using a calculator-interfaced voltage probe.

- **Form a Hypothesis** Students will calculate and predict reduction potentials for each half-cell pair.

- **Analyze the Results** Students will record data and establish a table of reduction potentials.

- **Draw Conclusions** Students will compare predicted reductions potentials with collected reduction potentials and calculate percentage error.

Teacher's Notes

MATERIALS AND EQUIPMENT

- Listed below are the quantities needed to prepare each of the solutions required for this experiment. Use distilled water for all solutions. The amounts shown are sufficient to fill three sets of 30 mL dropper bottles. This provides convenient dispensing for a class of 25 students.

  1.0 M $CuSO_4$ (M_1^{2+}) (24.96 g solid $CuSO_4 \cdot 5H_2O$ per 100 mL)
  1.0 M $ZnSO_4$ (M_2^{2+}) (26.95 g solid $ZnSO_4 \cdot 6H_2O$ per 100 mL)
  1.0 M $Pb(NO_3)_2$ (M_3^{2+}) (33.10 g solid $Pb(NO_3)_2$ per 100 mL)
  1.0 M $AgNO_3$ (M_4^+) (16.99 g solid $AgNO_3$ per 100 mL)
  1.0 M $FeSO_4$ (M_5^{2+}) (27.80 g solid $FeSO_4 \cdot 7H_2O$ per 100 mL)
  1.0 M $NaNO_3$ (8.50 g solid $NaNO_3$ per 100 mL)

- The micro-scale dimensions of this lab provide tremendous savings in quantities of reagents used in preparing 1.0 M solutions. Each student uses approximately 0.15 mL of each solution in preparing the voltaic cells; thus, the total amount of solution used for a class is less than 5 mL. A 30 mL dropper bottle of solution can be expected to last for several years. The micro-scale dimensions also allow you to use silver metal and 1.0 M $AgNO_3$ solution. The cost of such a macro-scale cell would normally be prohibitive.

- All of these solutions will store well except the 1.0 M $FeSO_4$. It is best to prepare this solution fresh each year.

- Store the 1.0 M $AgNO_3$ solution in an opaque or brown glass bottle. It should also be kept in a dark cabinet when not in use.

- Each of the metal pieces should be cut in sizes approximately 1 cm × 1 cm. Cut each of the metals into distinct shapes (square, triangle, trapezoid) in order to aid students in returning the proper metal to the proper container. The metals can be coded as follows:

$$M_1 = Cu; M_2 = Zn; M_3 = Pb; M_4 = Ag; M_5 = Fe$$

- The voltage calibration stored in the DataMate data-collection program will work fine for this experiment.

Graphing Calculator and Sensors
TIPS AND TRICKS

- Students should have the DataMate program loaded on their graphing calculators. Refer to Appendix B of Vernier's *Chemistry with Calculators* for instructions.

- Not all models of TI graphing calculators have the same amount of memory. If possible, instruct students to clear all calculator memory before loading the DataMate program.

Answers
ANALYSIS

1. Metal M_4 (Ag/Ag^+) had the highest reduction potential. Metal M_2 (Zn/Zn^{2+}) had the lowest reduction potential.

2. The combination of metals M_2 / M_4 (Zn/Ag) yielded a measured potential of 1.49 V.

3. The identity of each of the metals is listed below along with the measured reduction potentials and the accepted reduction potentials from the Table of Standard Reduction Potentials. Most of the metals should easily be identified with the exception of iron, which may be mistaken for nickel.

Metal	Experiment reduction potential (E°)	Standard reduction potential (E°)
M_2 (Zn)	−0.74 V	−0.76 V
M_5 (Fe)	−0.30 V	−0.44 V
M_3 (Pb)	−0.13 V	−0.13 V
M_1 (Cu)	+0.34 V	+0.34 V
M_4 (Ag)	+0.79 V	+0.80 V

CONCLUSIONS

1. The substitution of gold for silver would have increased the cell potential for all combinations in this experiment. The metal gold (Au) has a reduction potential of +1.50 V, which is higher than silver (Ag) with a reduction potential of +0.80 V.

2. An electrochemical cell using Ag and Zn should yield a standard potential of +1.56 V. If four cells were connected in series, the result would be a voltage of +6.24 V.

DATA TABLES WITH SAMPLE DATA
DATA TABLE 1

Voltaic cell (metals used)	Measured potential (V)	Metal number of (+) lead	Metal number of (−) lead
M_1 / M_2	1.08 V	M_1	M_2
M_1 / M_3	0.47 V	M_1	M_3
M_1 / M_4	0.45 V	M_4	M_1
M_1 / M_5	0.64 V	M_1	M_5

DATA TABLE 2

	Predicted potential (V)	Measured potential (V)	Percentage error (%)
M_2 / M_3	$-0.47 - (-1.08) = 0.61$ V	0.60 V	1.6 %
M_2 / M_4	$0.45 - (-1.08) = 1.53$ V	1.49 V	2.6 %
M_2 / M_5	$-0.64 - (-1.08) = 0.44$ V	0.46 V	4.5 %
M_3 / M_4	$0.45 - (-0.47) = 0.92$ V	0.90 V	2.2 %
M_3 / M_5	$-0.47 - (-0.64) = 0.17$ V	0.16 V	5.9 %
M_4 / M_5	$0.45 - (-0.64) = 1.09$ V	1.07 V	1.8 %

DATA TABLE 3

Metal (M_x)	Lowest (−) reduction potential, E° (V)
M_2 (Zn/Zn^{2+})	−1.08 V
M_5 (Fe/Fe^{2+})	−0.64 V
M_3 (Pb/Pb^{2+})	−0.47 V
M_1 (Cu/Cu^{2+})	0.00 V
M_4 (Ag/Ag$^+$)	+0.45 V
	Highest (+) reduction potential, E° (V)

Name _____ Class _____ Date _____

Skills Practice Lab)   **PROBEWARE LAB**

Micro-Voltaic Cells

Your small plane has just crashed on a remote island in the South Pacific. After recovering from the crash, you inventory the plane's contents. The only useful item still working in the plane is the radio, but the plane's battery has been completely destroyed, and you have no other means of powering the radio. Wandering around the island, you discover a small building that appears to be an abandoned research facility. Inside you discover a working gasoline generator and a laboratory filled with chemicals and various items of lab equipment, but no batteries. Upon careful consideration, you decide that there is no way to get the generator to the radio or the radio to the lab. You decide that your best bet is to construct a new battery.

In one of the cabinets, you discover a collection of metal strips and solutions. The writing is in a foreign language with which you are unfamiliar. It is apparent from the writing that certain metals correspond to certain solutions. Remembering a little about electrochemistry from your high school chemistry class, you decide that you can use the metal strips and solutions to build an electrochemical cell. You realize that before you can begin, you need to establish a table of reduction potentials in order to choose the proper metals for the anode and cathode of the cell. After further searching, you discover a working voltmeter and all the materials necessary to create a series of micro-voltaic cells using the unknown metals and solutions.

In this experiment, you will be using a calculator-interfaced voltage probe in place of a voltmeter. The (+) lead makes contact with one metal and the (−) lead with another. If a positive voltage appears on the calculator screen, the cell has been connected correctly. If the voltage reading is negative, switch the positions of the leads. The metal attached to the (+) lead is the cathode (where reduction takes place) and thus has a higher, more positive, reduction potential. The metal attached to the (−) lead is the anode (where oxidation takes place) and has the lower, more negative, reduction potential.

OBJECTIVES

- **Measure** potential differences between various pairs of half-cells.

- **Predict** potentials of half-cell combinations.

- **Compare** measured cell potentials with predicted cell potentials.

- **Calculate** percentage error for measured potentials.

- **Establish** the reduction potentials for five unknown metals.

Name _____ Class _____ Date _____

Micro-Voltaic Cells *continued*

MATERIALS

- filter paper, 11.0 cm diameter
- metals M_1, M_2, M_3, M_4, and M_5, 1×1 cm each
- $NaNO_3$, 1 M
- sandpaper
- solutions of M_1^{2+}, M_2^{2+}, . . . , and M_5^{2+}, 1 M each

EQUIPMENT

- forceps
- glass plate, 15×15 cm, or Petri dish, 11.5 cm diameter
- LabPro or CBL2 interface
- TI graphing calculator
- voltage probe

SAFETY

- Wear safety goggles when working around chemicals, acids, bases, flames, or heating devices.
- If any substance gets in your eyes, notify your instructor immediately and flush your eyes with running water for at least 15 minutes.
- If a chemical is spilled on the floor or lab bench, alert your instructor, but do not clean it up unless your instructor says it is OK to do so.
- Secure loose clothing, and remove dangling jewelry. Do not wear open-toed shoes or sandals in the lab.
- Wear an apron or lab coat to protect your clothing when working with chemicals.
- Never return unused chemicals to the original container; follow instructions for proper disposal.
- Always use caution when working with chemicals.
- Never mix chemicals unless specifically directed to do so.
- Never taste, touch, or smell chemicals unless specifically directed to do so.

Procedure

EQUIPMENT PREPARATION

1. Obtain and wear goggles.
2. Plug the voltage probe into Channel 1 of the LabPro or CBL 2 interface. Use the link cable to connect the TI graphing calculator to the interface. Firmly press in the cable ends.
3. Turn on the calculator, and start the DATAMATE program. Press [CLEAR] to reset the program.

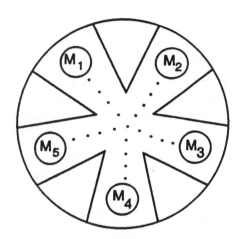

FIGURE 1

4. Set up the calculator and interface for the voltage probe.

    a. If the calculator displays VOLTAGE (V) in CH 1, proceed directly to Step 5. If it does not, continue with this step to set up your sensor manually.

    b. Select SETUP from the main screen.

    c. Press ⎡ENTER⎤ to select CH 1.

    d. Select the voltage probe you are using from the SELECT SENSOR menu.

    e. Select OK to return to the main screen.

5. Obtain a piece of filter paper, and draw five small circles with connecting lines, as shown in **Figure 1.** Using a pair of scissors, cut wedges between the circles as shown. Label the circles M_1, M_2, M_3, M_4, and M_5. Place the filter paper on top of the glass plate.

6. Obtain five pieces of metal, "M_1," "M_2," "M_3," "M_4," and "M_5." Sand each piece of metal on both sides. Place each metal near the circle with the same number.

7. Place three drops of each solution on its circle (M_1^{2+} on M_1, etc.). Then place the piece of metal on the wet spot with its respective cation. The top side of the metal should be kept dry. Then add several drops of 1 M $NaNO_3$ to the line drawn between each circle and the center of the filter paper. Be sure there is a continuous trail of $NaNO_3$ between each circle and the center. You may have to periodically dampen the filter paper with $NaNO_3$ during the experiment. **CAUTION:** *Handle these solutions with care. Some are poisonous, and some cause hard-to-remove stains. If a spill occurs, ask your teacher how to clean it up safely.*

| Micro-Voltaic Cells *continued*

DATA COLLECTION

8. Use metal M_1 (the one that is obviously copper) as the reference metal. Determine the potential of four cells by connecting M_1 to M_2, M_1 to M_3, M_1 to M_4, and M_1 to M_5. This is done by bringing the (+) lead in contact with one metal and the (–) lead in contact with the other. If the voltage displayed on the main screen of the calculator is (–), then reverse the leads. Wait about five seconds to take a voltage reading, and record the (+) value appearing on the calculator screen in Table 1 (round to the nearest 0.01 V). Also record which metal is the (+) terminal and which is (–), when the voltage value is positive. Use the same procedure and measure the potential of the other three cells, continuing to use M_1 as the reference electrode.

DATA TABLE 1

Voltaic cell (metals used)	Measured potential (V)	Metal number of (+) lead	Metal number of (–) lead
M_1 / M_2			
M_1 / M_3			
M_1 / M_4			
M_1 / M_5			

9. Go to Step 1 of Processing the Data. Use the method described in Step 1 to rank the five metals from the lowest (–) reduction potential to the highest (+) reduction potential. Then *predict* the potentials for the remaining six cell combinations.

10. Now return to your work station and *measure* the potential of the six remaining half-cell combinations. If the $NaNO_3$ salt bridge solution has dried, you may have to re-moisten it. Record each measured potential in Table 2.

DATA TABLE 2

	Predicted potential (V)	Measured potential (V)	Percentage error (%)
M_2 / M_3			
M_2 / M_4			
M_2 / M_5			
M_3 / M_4			
M_3 / M_5			
M_4 / M_5			

Name _____ Class _____ Date _____

Micro-Voltaic Cells *continued*

11. When you are finished, select QUIT and exit the DATAMATE program.

12. When you have finished, use forceps to remove each of the pieces of metal from the filter paper. Rinse each piece of metal with tap water. Dry it, and return it to the correct container. Remove the filter paper from the glass plate using the forceps, and discard it as directed by your teacher. Rinse the glass plate with tap water, making sure that your hands do not come in contact with wet spots on the glass.

PROCESSING THE DATA

1. After finishing Step 8 in the procedure, arrange the five metals (including M_1) in Data Table 2 from the lowest reduction potential at the top (most negative) to the highest reduction potential at the bottom (most positive). Metal M_1, the standard reference, will be given an arbitrary value of 0.00 V. If the other metal was correctly connected to the *negative* terminal, it will be placed *above* M_1 in the chart (with a negative $E°$ value). If it was connected to the positive terminal, it will be placed below M_1 in the chart (with a positive $E°$ value). The numerical value of the potential relative to M_1 will simply be the value that you measured. Record your results in Table 3.

DATA TABLE 3

Metal (M$_x$)	Lowest (–) reduction potential, E° (V)
	Highest (+) reduction potential, E° (V)

Then calculate the *predicted* potential of each of the remaining cell combinations shown in Table 2, using the reduction potentials you just determined (in Table 3). Record the predicted cell potentials in Table 2. Return to Step 10 in the procedure, and finish the experiment.

2. Calculate the percentage error for each of the potentials you measured in Step 11 of the procedure. Do this by comparing the measured cell potentials with the predicted cell potentials in Table 2.

Name _____ Class _____ Date _____

Micro-Voltaic Cells *continued*

Analysis

1. Examining data Which metal had the highest reduction potential? Which had

the lowest reduction potential? _____

_____

_____

2. Examining data Which combination of metals had the largest measured cell

potential? _____

_____

_____

3. Analyzing results In Step 8 the metal M_1 was arbitrarily given a reduction potential of 0.00 V and used as the reference metal in determining the potential of each voltaic cell. The metal M_1 can be positively identified as being copper. According to the Table of Standard Reduction Potentials, Cu has a reduction potential of +0.34 V. Adjust all of the reduction potentials in Table 3 by adding +0.34 V. Use the Table of Standard Reduction Potentials found in your textbook to properly identify each of the unknown metals in Table 3.

Conclusions

1. Drawing conclusions If metal M_4 was actually gold, would your measured

cell potential had been higher or lower? Explain why. _____

_____

_____

_____

_____

2. Inferring conclusions If the battery back in the plane requires a 6 V power source, how can you arrange the electrochemical cell to yield the necessary

voltage? _____

_____

_____

_____

_____

Answer Key

Concept Review: Oxidation-Reduction Reactions

1. a
2. c
3. b
4. e
5. d
6. g
7. f
8. Zn: +2, Cl: −1
9. S: +6, O: −2
10. H: +1, N: +5, O: −2
11. Al: +3, S: +6, O: −2
12. Pb: +2, O: −2
13. C: +4, O: −2
14. H: +1, S: +6, O: −2
15. $H_2O_2(aq) + 2H^+(aq) + 2e^- \rightarrow 2H_2O(l)$
16. oxidation, reduction, $2Mg + O_2$ $\rightarrow 2Mg^{2+} + 2O^{2-}$; $Mg + O_2 - 2MgO$
17. $2MnO_4^- + 5SO_2 + 2H_2O \rightarrow 2Mn^{2+} + 5SO_4^{2-} + 4H^+$
18. $2NO_3^- + 3Cu + 8H^+ \rightarrow 2NO + 3Cu^{2+} + 4H_2O$
19. $8H_2S + 16NO_3^- + 16H^+ \rightarrow 16NO_2 + S_8 + 16H_2O$
20. K is oxidized and Cl is reduced.

Concept Review: Introduction to Electrochemistry

1. voltage
2. electric current, ampere
3. electrode
4. electrochemical
5. c
6. b
7. e
8. d
9. f
10. a
11. h
12. g
13. cathode
14. electrolyte
15. oxidation
16. reduction

17. salt bridge or porous barrier
18. Electrons flow from the higher "pressure" in the negative terminal through a metal circuit, which includes the light blub, towards the positive terminal.
19. $Zn(s) \rightarrow Zn^{2+}(aq) + 2e^-$, anode
20. $Cu^{2+}(aq) + 2e^- \rightarrow Cu(s)$, reduction

Concept Review: Galvanic Cells

1. simple
2. two, outside, two, thin
3. indirectly, inefficient
4. directly, simple, efficient
5. possible
6. galvanic
7. chemical, electrical
8. portable
9. acidic
10. alkaline
11. carbon
12. alkaline
13. steel
14. lead
15. lead(II) sulfate
16. galvanic, electrolytic
17. rechargeable
18. galvanic
19. Daniell
20. Ag, cathode; Zn, anode; +1.5614 V
21. Cu, cathode; Pb, anode; +0.4681 V
22. $Zn(s) + Cu^{2+}(aq) \xrightarrow{2e^-} Zn^{2+}(aq) + Cu(s)$, spontaneously to the right
    $\Delta E = (0.34) + (+0.76) = 1.10$ V
23. $I_2(s) + 2Cl^-(aq) \xrightarrow{2e^-} Cl_2(g) + 2I^-(aq)$ spontaneously to the left
    $\Delta E = (-0.54) + (1.36) = 0.82$ V
24. $2Ag^+(aq) + Cu(s) \xrightarrow{2e^-} Cu^{2+}(aq) + 2Ag(s)$ spontaneously to the right
    $\Delta E = (0.80) + (-0.34) = 0.46$ V
25. the deterioration of metals due to oxidation reactions with their environment
26. oxygen, water, and ions

27. The more active metal provides an anodic region and the less active metal provides a cathodic region; plumbing leaks occur where steel and copper water pipes are joined.

28. A metal that is more easily oxidized is attached to a metallic structure so that it serves as an anode, preventing the corrosion of the structural metal.

Concept Review: Electrolytic Cells

1. Electrolytic, nonspontaneous, electrical

2. electrolysis, molten, Downs, Downs cell

3. released, oxidation, consumed, reduction, anode, cathode

4. positive, negative

5. electrosynthesis

6. $2Na^+(l) + 2e^- \rightarrow 2Na(l)$

7. $2Cl^-(l) \rightarrow 2e^- + Cl_2(g)$

8. $2Na^+(l) + 2Cl^-(l) \xrightarrow{e} 2Na(l) + Cl_2(g)$

9. Reduction

10. anode

11. oxygen, hydrogen

12. electrolyte

13. refine

14. electrical, chemical

15. d

16. b

17. f

18. h

19. c

20. a

21. g

22. e

Additional Problems

REDOX EQUATIONS

1. $3Mg + N_2 \rightarrow Mg_3N_2$

2. $SO_2 + Br_2 + 2H_2O \rightarrow 2HBr + H_2SO_4$

3. $H_2S + Cl_2 \rightarrow S + 2HCl$

4. $PbO_2 + 4HBr \rightarrow PbBr_2 + Br_2 + 2H_2O$

5. $S + 6HNO_3 \rightarrow 6NO_2 + H_2SO_4 + 2H_2O$

6. $NaIO_3 + N_2H_4 + 2HCl \rightarrow N_2 + NaICl_2 + 3H_2O$

7. $MnO_2 + H_2O_2 + 2HCl \rightarrow MnCl_2 + O_2 + 2H_2O$

8. $3AsH_3 + 4NaClO_3 \rightarrow 3H_3AsO_4 + 4NaCl$

9. $K_2Cr_2O_7 + 3H_2C_2O_4 + 8HCl \rightarrow 2CrCl_3 + 6CO_2 + 2KCl + 7H_2O$

10. $2Hg(NO_3)_2 \rightarrow 2HgO + 4NO_2 + O_2$

11. $4HAuCl_4 + 3N_2H_4 \rightarrow 4Au + 3N_2 + 16HCl$

12. $5Sb_2(SO_4)_3 + 4KMnO_4 + 24H_2O \rightarrow 10H_3SbO_4 + 2K_2SO_4 + 4MnSO_4 + 9H_2SO_4$

13. $3Mn(NO_3)_2 + 5NaBiO_3 + 9HNO_3 \rightarrow 5Bi(NO_3)_2 + 3HMnO_4 + 5NaNO_3 + 3H_2O$

14. $H_3AsO_4 + 4Zn + 8HCl \rightarrow AsH_3 + 4ZnCl_2 + 4H_2O$

15. $KClO_3 + 6HCl \rightarrow 3Cl_2 + 3H_2O + KCl$

16. $2KClO_3 + 4HCl \rightarrow Cl_2 + 2ClO_2 + 2H_2O + 2KCl$

17. $2MnCl_3 + 2H_2O \rightarrow MnCl_2 + MnO_2 + 4HCl$

18. $2NaOH + 6H_2O + 2Al \rightarrow 2NaAl(OH)_4 + 3H_2$

19. $6Br_2 + 6Ca(OH)_2 \rightarrow 5CaBr_2 + Ca(BrO_3)_2 + 6H_2O$

20. $N_2O + 2NaClO + 2NaOH \rightarrow 2NaCl + 2NaNO_2 + H_2O$

21. $4HBr + MnO_2 \rightarrow MnBr_2 + 2H_2O + Br_2$

22. $Au + 4HCl + HNO_3 \rightarrow HAuCl_4 + NO + 2H_2O$

ELECTROCHEMISTRY

1. $E^0 = +2.77$ V; spontaneous

2. $E^0 = +1.11$ V; spontaneous

3. $E^0 = -0.46$ V; not spontaneous

4. $E^0 = +1.50$ V; spontaneous

5. $E^0 = +2.46$ V; spontaneous

6. $E^0 = +1.28$ V; spontaneous

7. $E^0 = +3.71$ V; spontaneous

8. $E^0 = -3.41$ V; not spontaneous

9. $E^0 = +1.32$ V; spontaneous

10. $E^0 = -3.60$ V; not spontaneous

11. Overall reaction:
$Cl_2 + Ni \rightarrow Ni^{2+} + 2Cl^-$
Cathode reaction: $Cl_2 + 2e^- \rightarrow 2Cl^-$
Anode reaction: $Ni \rightarrow Ni^{2+} + 2e^-$
Cell voltage: $+1.62$ V

12. Overall reaction:
$3Hg^{2+} + 2Fe \rightarrow 3Hg + 2Fe^{3+}$
Cathode reaction: $Hg^{2+} + 2e^- \rightarrow Hg$
Anode reaction: $Fe \rightarrow Fe^{3+} + 3e^-$
Cell voltage: $+0.89$ V

13. Overall reaction:

$3MnO_4^- + Al \rightarrow 3MnO_4^{2-} + Al^{3+}$

Cathode reaction:

$MnO_4^- + e^- \rightarrow MnO_4^{2-}$

Anode reaction: $Al \rightarrow Al^{3+} + 3e^-$

Cell voltage: $+2.22$ V

14. Overall reaction:

$2MnO_4^- + 6H^+ + 5H_2S \rightarrow$
$2Mn^{2+} + 8H_2O + 5S$

Cathode reaction:

$MnO_4^- + 8H^+ + 5e^- \rightarrow Mn^{2+} + 4H_2O$

Anode reaction: $H_2S \rightarrow S + 2H^+ + 2e^-$

Cell voltage: $+1.36$ V

15. Overall reaction:

$Ca^{2+} + 2Li \rightarrow Ca + 2Li^+$

Cathode reaction: $Ca^{2+} + 2e^- \rightarrow Ca$

Anode reaction: $Li \rightarrow Li^+ + e^-$

Cell voltage: $+0.17$ V

16. Overall reaction:

$2MnO_4^- + 16H^+ + 10Br^- \rightarrow$
$2Mn^{2+} + 8H_2O + 5Br_2$

Cathode reaction:

$MnO_4^- + 8H^+ + 5e^- \rightarrow$
$Mn^{2+} + 4H_2O$

Anode reaction: $2Br^- \rightarrow Br_2 + 2e^-$

Cell voltage: $+0.43$ V

17. Overall reaction:

$2Fe^{3+} + Sn \rightarrow 2Fe^{2+} + Sn^{2+}$

Cathode reaction: $Fe^{3+} + e^- \rightarrow Fe^{2+}$

Anode reaction: $Sn \rightarrow Sn^{2+} + 2e^-$

Cell voltage: $+0.91$ V

18. Overall reaction:

$Cr_2O_7^{2-} + 14H^+ + 3Zn \rightarrow$
$2Cr^{3+} + 7H_2O + 3Zn^{2+}$

Cathode reaction:

$Cr_2O_7^{2-} + 14H^+ + 6e^- \rightarrow$
$2Cr^{3+} + 7H_2O$

Anode reaction: $Zn \rightarrow Zn^{2+} + 2e^-$

Cell voltage: $+1.99$ V

19. Overall reaction:

$Ba + Ca^{2+} \rightarrow Ba^{2+} + Ca$

Cathode reaction: $Ca^{2+} + 2e^- \rightarrow Ca$

Anode reaction: $Ba \rightarrow Ba^{2+} + 2e^-$

Cell voltage: $+0.04$ V

20. Overall reaction:

$Cd + Hg_2^{2+} \rightarrow Cd^{2+} + 2Hg$

Cathode reaction: $Hg_2^{2+} + 2e^- \rightarrow 2Hg$

Anode reaction: $Cd \rightarrow Cd^{2+} + 2e^-$

Cell voltage: $+1.20$ V

Answer Key

Quiz—Section: Oxidation-Reduction Reactions

1. a	**6.** b
2. b	**7.** a
3. c	**8.** b
4. d	**9.** d
5. c	**10.** b

Quiz—Section: Introduction to Electrochemistry

1. b	**6.** a
2. c	**7.** b
3. d	**8.** a
4. a	**9.** c
5. c	**10.** d

Quiz—Section: Galvanic Cells

1. a	**6.** a
2. b	**7.** c
3. d	**8.** d
4. d	**9.** a
5. c	**10.** a

Quiz—Section: Electrolytic Cells

1. a	**6.** b
2. a	**7.** d
3. b	**8.** c
4. a	**9.** b
5. d	**10.** a

Chapter Test

1. d	**11.** c
2. b	**12.** c
3. c	**13.** a
4. b	**14.** c
5. c	**15.** a
6. d	**16.** c
7. d	**17.** a
8. b	**18.** b
9. c	**19.** c
10. d	**20.** c

21. An electrolytic cell uses electric current to complete a chemical reaction. A galvanic cell uses a chemical reaction to generate an electric current.

22. Answers will vary. Most students should list the anode, cathode, and electrolyte as features common to all batteries. The anode and cathode are necessary to form an electrochemical cell as well as for external connections and the electrolyte is necessary for the electrochemical cell to function. Other items could include the case, terminals, and a porous barrier.

23. Reduction absorbs electrons to change an ion into an element or into an ion with a reduced oxidation number. The electrons for this process must come from a source, which is an oxidation. Oxidation is a process that releases electrons to produce ions of greater oxidation number. Energy and mass must be conserved, so both processes must occur together.

24. $E°_{cell} = +0.46$ V

25. Anode: $Zn \rightarrow Zn^{2+} + 2e^-$
Cathode: $Hg^{2+} + 2e^- \rightarrow Hg$

Oxidation, Reduction, and Electrochemistry

MULTIPLE CHOICE

1. The loss of one or more electrons from an atom is called
   a. oxidation
   b. reduction
   c. electrochemistry
   d. half-reaction

   Answer: A   Difficulty: I   Section: 1   Objective: 1

2. The gain of electrons is called
   a. oxidation.
   b. reduction.
   c. electrochemistry.
   d. half-reaction.

   Answer: B   Difficulty: I   Section: 1   Objective: 1

3. A single reaction where oxidation and reduction take place is called
   a. a half-reaction.
   b. electrochemistry.
   c. a redox reaction.
   d. a double oxidation.

   Answer: C   Difficulty: I   Section: 1   Objective: 1

4. The oxidation number of a monatomic ion is equal to
   a. the charge on the ion.
   b. zero.
   c. the sum of all the oxidation numbers.
   d. the oxidation number of an oxygen atom.

   Answer: A   Difficulty: I   Section: 1   Objective: 2

5. Which is the most electronegative element?
   a. oxygen
   b. hydrogen
   c. zinc
   d. fluorine

   Answer: D   Difficulty: I   Section: 1   Objective: 2

6. The part of a reaction that involves only oxidation or reduction is a(n)
   a. redox reaction.
   b. electron transfer.
   c. chemical reaction.
   d. half-reaction.

   Answer: D   Difficulty: I   Section: 1   Objective: 4

7. Substances that cause the oxidation of other substances are
   a. reducing agents.
   b. catalysts.
   c. oxidizing agents.
   d. cells.

   Answer: C   Difficulty: I   Section: 1   Objective: 2

8. If the reactants in a spontaneous energy-releasing redox reaction are connected externally by a wire conductor, the energy is released in the form of
   a. light.
   b. electrical energy.
   c. sound.
   d. mechanical energy.

   Answer: B   Difficulty: I   Section: 2   Objective: 1

9. In which system does a spontaneous redox reaction generate electrical energy?
   a. galvanic cell
   b. electrolytic cell
   c. electroplating cell
   d. half-cell

   Answer: A   Difficulty: II   Section: 3   Objective: 1

10. In a zinc-carbon dry cell, oxidation of
    a. zinc occurs at the anode.
    b. manganese occurs at the anode.
    c. zinc occurs at the cathode.
    d. manganese occurs at the cathode.

    Answer: A   Difficulty: II   Section: 3   Objective: 1

11. In a zinc-carbon dry cell,
    a. the zinc electrode is the cathode and the carbon electrode is the anode.
    b. the zinc electrode is the anode and the carbon electrode is the cathode.
    c. both electrodes are auto-oxidizing and serve as both cathodes and anodes.
    d. neither electrode can be considered a cathode or an anode.

    Answer: B   Difficulty: I   Section: 3   Objective: 1

12. .Where does oxidation take place in an electrochemical cell?
    a. the anode
    b. the cathode
    c. the anode or the cathode
    d. the half-cell

    Answer: A   Difficulty: I   Section: 2   Objective: 2

13. Where does reduction take place in an electrochemical cell?
    a. the anode
    b. the cathode
    c. the anode or the cathode
    d. the half-cell

    Answer: B   Difficulty: I   Section: 2   Objective:2

14. An electrode reaction is reduction. This means that the electrode is a(n)
    a. cathode.
    b. anode.
    c. electrochemical cell.
    d. electrolytic cell.

    Answer: A   Difficulty: I   Section: 2   Objective: 3

15. An electrochemical cell that generates electrical energy is a(n)
    a. electroplating cell.
    b. electrolysis cell.
    c. electrolytic cell.
    d. galvanic cell.

    Answer: D   Difficulty: I   Section: 3   Objective: 1

16. If the reactants in a galvanic cell are in contact,
    a. most of the energy is released as an electric current.
    b. most of the energy is released as heat.
    c. oxidation and reduction do not occur.
    d. hydrogen gas is released.

    Answer: B   Difficulty: II   Section: 3   Objective: 1

17. Electrons in a galvanic cell normally flow
    a. from cathode to anode.
    b. through a porous barrier.
    c. in both directions through the external circuit.
    d. from anode to cathode.

    Answer: D   Difficulty: I   Section: 3   Objective: 1

18. For electrons to flow in a galvanic cell, the two half-cells must be
    a. connected by a wire and a porous barrier.
    b. completely isolated from one another.
    c. in the same solution.
    d. connected to a dry cell.

    Answer: A   Difficulty: II   Section: 3   Objective: 1

19. The deterioration of metals is called
    a. combustion.
    b. decomposition.
    c. corrosion.
    d. electronegativity.

    Answer: C   Difficulty: I   Section: 3   Objective: 2

20. What is *not* needed for corrosion of metals?
    a. oxygen
    b. ions
    c. water
    d. sunlight
    Answer: D   Difficulty: I   Section: 3   Objective: 2

21. A more positive value for electrode potential means the electrode is more likely to be a(n)
    a. anode.
    b. cathode.
    c. electrolytic cell.
    d. electrochemical cell.
    Answer: B   Difficulty: I   Section: 3   Objective: 3

22. In which cell does a current drive a nonspontaneous redox reaction?
    a. electrolytic cell
    b. dry cell
    c. fuel cell
    d. galvanic cell
    Answer: A   Difficulty: I   Section: 4   Objective: 1

23. In an electrolytic cell, reduction occurs
    a. at the cathode.
    b. at the anode.
    c. at either the cathode or the anode.
    d. between the cathode and the anode.
    Answer: A   Difficulty: I   Section: 4   Objective: 1

24. Which process deposits metal onto a surface?
    a. electrolysis
    b. electroplating
    c. autoxidation
    d. oxidation
    Answer: B   Difficulty: I   Section: 4   Objective: 3

25. Electroplating is an application of which reaction?
    a. electrolytic reactions
    b. fuel cell reactions
    c. auto-oxidation reactions
    d. galvanic reactions
    Answer: A   Difficulty: I   Section: 4   Objective: 3

26. Electrical energy is converted into chemical energy within a(n)
    a. fuel cell reaction.
    b. galvanic cell.
    c. half-cell.
    d. electrolytic cell.
    Answer: D   Difficulty: II   Section: 4   Objective: 1

27. Pure water has too few ions to be conductive enough for electrolysis. Therefore, what must be added to water?
    a. anode sludge
    b. an electrode
    c. an electrolyte
    d. a fuel cell
    Answer: C   Difficulty: II   Section: 4   Objective: 2

28. What type of process is the electrolysis reaction?
    a. electrode reaction
    b. dry cell reaction
    c. spontaneous
    d. nonspontaneous
    Answer: D   Difficulty: I   Section: 4   Objective: 2

COMPLETION

29. Reduction is a chemical change that involves the gain of _____.
    Answer: electrons   Difficulty: I   Section: 1   Objective: 1

30. A(n)_____ is the number of electrons that are added or removed from an atom in a combined state to convert it to an elemental form.

    Answer: oxidation number

    Difficulty: I   Section: 1   Objective: 2

31. The oxidation number of each hydrogen atom in a compound is usually _____ .

    Answer: +1   Difficulty: I   Section: 1   Objective: 2

32. The oxidation of an oxygen atom is usually _____.

    Answer: -2   Difficulty: I   Section: 1   Objective: 2

33. If an atom is not oxidized or reduced during a redox reaction, the _____ does not change.

    Answer: oxidation number

    Difficulty: I   Section: 1   Objective: 3

34. The part of a reaction that involves only oxidation or reduction is a

    _____.

    Answer: half-reaction

    Difficulty: II   Section: 1   Objective: 4

35. The half-reaction method is one way to _____ redox equations.

    Answer: balance   Difficulty: I   Section: 1   Objective: 4

36. Electrolytic cells change _____ into chemical energy.

    Answer: electrical energy

    Difficulty: I   Section: 4   Objective: 1

37. The movement of electrons is described as _____.

    Answer: electric current

    Difficulty: I   Section: 2   Objective: 1

38. The term _____ represents the amount of work it would take to move an electric charge between two points.

    Answer: voltage   Difficulty: I   Section: 2   Objective: 1

39. An electrochemical cell consists of two electrodes separated by an _____.

    Answer: electrolyte   Difficulty: I   Section: 2   Objective: 2

40. A(n) _____ is a conductor used to establish electrical contact with a nonmetallic part of a circuit.

    Answer: electrode   Difficulty: II   Section: 2   Objective: 2

41. The _____ is the electrode on which oxidation occurs.

    Answer: anode   Difficulty: II   Section: 2   Objective: 2

42. Reactions on electrodes cannot happen unless the electrodes are _____.

    Answer: connected   Difficulty: I   Section: 2   Objective: 2

43. A galvanic cell can change _____ into electrical energy.

    Answer: chemical energy

    Difficulty: I   Section: 3   Objective: 1

44. In a _____, moist electrolyte pastes are used instead of solutions.

    Answer: dry cell (or battery)

    Difficulty: I   Section: 3   Objective: 1

45. A(n) _____ has a basic electrolyte.
     Answer: alkaline cell
     Difficulty: I   Section: 3   Objective: 1

46. Unlike dry cells, lead-acid cells are _____.
     Answer: rechargeable
     Difficulty: I   Section: 3   Objective: 1

47. Gold, the metal with the highest _____, is the most corrosion resistant.
     Answer: electronegativity
     Difficulty: I   Section: 3   Objective: 2

48. If the electrode potential of a cell is negative, the reaction can happen if
     _____ is added.
     Answer: energy   Difficulty: I   Section: 3   Objective: 3

49. An electrolytic cell _____ energy.
     Answer: consumes   Difficulty: I   Section: 4   Objective: 1

50. The process of _____ breaks a compound into its elements.
     Answer: electrolysis Difficulty: II   Section: 4   Objective: 2

51. The electrolysis of _____ is the largest single user of electrical energy in
     the United States.
     Answer: aluminum   Difficulty: II   Section: 4   Objective: 2

52. The electrolytic process of coating an object with a metal is called _____.
     Answer: electroplating
     Difficulty: I   Section: 4   Objective: 3

53. A major benefit of electroplating a metal is that it becomes more _____
     to corrosion.
     Answer: resistant   Difficulty: I   Section: 4   Objective: 3

54. A drawback of electroplating is that _____ can build up overtime in the
     solutions used for the process.
     Answer: impurities Difficulty: I   Section: 4   Objective: 3

55. Toxic metals, such as _____, can build up in the solution used for
     electroplating.
     Answer: cadmium or chromium
     Difficulty: I   Section: 4   Objective: 3

SHORT ANSWER

57. What is oxidation?
     Answer: The loss of one or more electrons.
     Difficulty: I   Section: 1   Objective: 1

58. What is reduction?
     Answer: The gain of electrons during a chemical reaction.
     Difficulty: I   Section: 1   Objective: 1

59. What is a redox reaction?
     Answer: A single reaction in which an oxidation and a reduction happen.
     Difficulty: I   Section: 1   Objective: 3

---

60. What can you tell by tracking oxidation numbers?

Answer: If an atom is oxidized or reduced.

Difficulty: II   Section: 1   Objective: 4

61. Describe the chemical reaction that occurs at the cathode.

Answer: The sample gains electrons, and reduction occurs.

Difficulty: II   Section: 2   Objective: 3

62. Describe the chemical reaction that occurs at the anode.

Answer: The sample loses electrons, and oxidation occurs.

Difficulty: II   Section: 2   Objective: 3

63. What is an electrode?

Answer: A conductor used to establish electrical contact with a nonmetallic part of a circuit.

Difficulty: I   Section: 2   Objective: 2

64. What is a cathode?

Answer: The electrode at which reduction occurs.

Difficulty: I   Section: 3   Objective: 1

65. In which direction do electrons flow in a galvanic cell?

Answer: Electrons flow from the anode to the cathode.

Difficulty: I   Section: 3   Objective: 1

66. Describe how a galvanic cell can drive a nonspontaneous chemical reaction.

Answer: The galvanic cell provides the energy to force electrons to move and drive a chemical process which is not spontaneous.

Difficulty: I   Section: 3   Objective: 2

67. Why are scientists experimenting with fuel cells in power plants?

Answer: Fuel cells directly change chemical energy into electrical energy. This makes them very efficient and cleaner than burning fossil fuels in power plants.

Difficulty: II   Section: 3   Objective: 1

68. What makes corrosion worse in some areas?

Answer: Some areas have higher ion concentrations from airborne salt near oceans, acidic air pollution, or salt spread on icy roads.

Difficulty: I   Section: 3   Objective: 2

69. Describe how sodium metal is produced.

Answer: Electrolysis of molten sodium chloride produces elemental sodium and chlorine.

Difficulty: I   Section: 4   Objective: 2

70. Write the anodic and cathodic reactions for the electrolysis of molten sodium chloride.

Answer:

Anode $2Cl^-(l) \rightarrow 2e^- + Cl_2(g)$

Cathode $2Na^+(l) + 2e^- \rightarrow 2Na(l)$

Difficulty: I   Section: 4   Objective: 2

71. Write the anodic and cathodic reactions for the electrolysis of water.

Answer:

Anode $6H_2O(l) \rightarrow 4e^- + O_2(g) + 4H_3O^+ (aq)$

Cathode $4H_2O(l) + 4e^- \rightarrow 2H_2(g) + 4OH^-(aq)$

Difficulty: I   Section: 4   Objective: 2

72. Describe electroplating.

Answer: This is the process of putting a thin layer of metal on a substance. The substance is made the cathode and placed in a solution of the metal that is being added.

Difficulty: I   Section: 4   Objective: 3

ESSAY QUESTIONS

73. Explain why most car batteries are lead-acid batteries.

Answer:

The lead-acid battery is very reliable and can economically give the large surges of electrical energy needed to start a cold engine.

Difficulty: II   Section: 3   Objective: 1

74. Compare the operation of a conventional power plant and a fuel cell.

Answer:

The power plant releases energy from a reaction as heat which is then converted into electrical energy. Fuel cells convert chemical energy directly to electrical energy.

Difficulty: II   Section: 3   Objective: 1

75. What observations suggest that a chemical reaction is occurring in a galvanic cell?

Answer:

Answers will vary. Some examples: electrical energy is generated, gas evolves at the electrodes, the color of the solution changes, the masses of the electrodes change.

Difficulty: II   Section: 3   Objective: 2

76. Describe the operation of an electrochemical cell.

Answer:

The electrochemical cell functions as a galvanic cell if the voltage applied is less than the equilibrium voltage. It functions as an electrolytic cell if the applied voltage is greater than the equilibrium voltage. It functions as an equilibrium cell if the applied voltage equals the equilibrium voltage

Difficulty: II   Section: 4   Objective: 1

PROBLEMS

77. Calculate the voltage of a cell composed of a copper electrode in a copper(II) solution and an aluminum electrode in a solution with aluminun ions.

Answer: $E^\circ_{cell} = E^\circ_{red} - E^\circ_{oxd}$
   $E^\circ_{cell} = +0.342 \text{ V} - (-1.66\text{V})$
   $E^\circ_{cell} = +2.00 \text{ V}$

Difficulty: II   Section: 3   Objective: 3

78. Calculate the voltage of a cell composed of a lead electrode in a lead (II) solution and a silver electrode in a solution with silver ions.

Answer: $E^\circ_{cell} = E^\circ_{red} - E^\circ_{oxd}$
   $E^\circ_{cell} = +0.80\text{V} - (-0.13\text{V})$
   $E^\circ_{cell} = +0.93 \text{ V}$

Difficulty: II   Section: 3   Objective: 3

Solutions Manual

Solutions for problems can also be found at go.hrw.com. Enter the keyword HW4ELETNS to obtain solutions.

Practice Problems A

1. a. Given: NH_4^+

Unknown: oxidation number for each atom

The oxidation number of the H atoms is +1. The oxidation number of the N atom is unknown.

$$\overset{x}{N}\overset{+1}{H_4^+}$$

Total oxidation number: $x + 4(+1) = +1$.

The oxidation number of the N atom is –3.

b. Given: Al

Unknown: oxidation number for each atom

Al represents a free element in atomic form, so the oxidation number of the Al atom is 0.

c. Given: H_2O

Unknown: oxidation number for each atom

The oxidation number of the H atoms is +1. The oxidation number of the O atom is –2.

Total oxidation number: $2(+1) + (-2) = 0$.

d. Given: Pb^{2+}

Unknown: oxidation number for each atom

Pb^{2+} is a monatomic ion, so the oxidation number is equal to the charge. The oxidation number of the Pb atom is +2.

e. Given: H_2

Unknown: oxidation number for each atom

H_2 represents a free element in molecular form, so the oxidation number of the H atoms is 0.

f. Given: $PbSO_4$

Unknown: oxidation number for each atom

The oxidation number of the O atoms is –2. The monatomic lead ion in $PbSO_4$ has a 2+ charge, so the oxidation number of the Pb atom is +2. The oxidation number of the S atom is unknown.

$$\overset{+2}{Pb}\overset{x}{S}\overset{-2}{O_4}$$

Total oxidation number: $(+2) + x + 4(-2) = 0$.

The oxidation number of the S atom is +6.

g. Given: $KClO_3$

Unknown: oxidation number for each atom

The oxidation number of the K atom is +1 because it is an atom of an element in Group 1. The oxidation number of the O atoms is –2. The oxidation number of the Cl atom is unknown.

$$\overset{+1}{K}\overset{x}{Cl}\overset{-2}{O_3}$$

Total oxidation number: $(+1) + x + 3(-2) = 0$.

The oxidation number of the Cl atom is +5.

h. Given: BF_3

Unknown: oxidation number for each atom

The oxidation number of the F atoms is -1. The oxidation number of the B atom is unknown.

$$\overset{x\,-1}{BF_3}$$

Total oxidation number: $x + 3(-1) = 0$.

The oxidation number of the B atom is $+3$.

i. Given: $Ca(OH)_2$

Unknown: oxidation number for each atom

The oxidation number of the Ca atom is $+2$ because it is an atom of an element in Group 2. The oxidation number of the O atoms is -2. The oxidation number of the H atoms is $+1$.

Total oxidation number: $(+2) + 2(-2) + 2(+1) = 0$.

j. Given: $Fe_2(CO_3)_3$

Unknown: oxidation number for each atom

Each iron ion has a 3+ charge, so the oxidation number of the Fe atoms is $+3$. The oxidation number of the O atoms is -2. The oxidation number of the C atoms is unknown.

$$\overset{+3\quad x\,-2}{Fe_2(CO_3)_3}$$

Total oxidation number: $2(+3) + 3(x) + 9(-2) = 0$.

The oxidation number of the C atoms is $+4$.

k. Given: $H_2PO_4^-$

Unknown: oxidation number for each atom

The oxidation number of the H atoms is $+1$. The oxidation number of the O atoms is -2. The oxidation number of the P atom is unknown.

$$\overset{+1\ \ x\,-2}{H_2PO_4^-}$$

Total oxidation number: $2(+1) + x + 4(-2) = -1$.

The oxidation number of the P atom is $+5$.

l. Given: NH_4NO_3

Unknown: oxidation number for each atom

With two polyatomic ions, consider each ion individually. In NH_4^+, the oxidation number of the H atoms is $+1$. The oxidation number of the N atom is unknown.

$$\overset{x\ +1}{NH_4^+}$$

Total oxidation number: $x + 4(+1) = +1$.

The oxidation number of the N atom in NH_4^+ is -3.

In NO_3^-, the oxidation number of the O atoms is -2. The oxidation number of the N atom is unknown.

$$\overset{x\ -2}{NO_3^-}$$

Total oxidation number: $x + 3(-2) = -1$.

The oxidation number of the N atom is NO_3^- is $+5$.

Practice Problems B

1. Given: $Fe(s) + O_2(aq) \rightarrow$ Unbalanced: $Fe \rightarrow Fe^{3+}$ $\qquad\qquad O_2 \rightarrow H_2O$
$\qquad Fe^{3+}(aq) + H_2O(l)$ Balance O: $Fe \rightarrow Fe^{3+}$ $\qquad\qquad O_2 \rightarrow 2H_2O$

Unknown: balanced Balance H: $Fe \rightarrow Fe^{3+}$ $\qquad\qquad 4H_3O^+ + O_2 \rightarrow 6H_2O$
$\qquad$ equation Balance e^-: $Fe \rightarrow Fe^{3+} + 3e^-$ $\qquad 4e^- + 4H_3O^+ + O_2 \rightarrow 6H_2O$

$$4[Fe \rightarrow Fe^{3+} + 3e^-]$$
$$\underline{3[4e^- + 4H_3O^+ + O_2 \rightarrow 6H_2O]}$$
$$4Fe + 12H_3O^+ + 3O_2 \rightarrow 4Fe^{3+} + 18H_2O$$

2. Given: $Al(s) + H_3O^+(aq)$ Unbalanced: $Al \rightarrow Al^{3+}$ $\qquad\qquad H_3O^+ \rightarrow H_2$
$\qquad \rightarrow Al^{3+}(aq) + H_2(g)$ Balance O: $Al \rightarrow Al^{3+}$ $\qquad\qquad H_3O^+ \rightarrow H_2 + H_2O$

Unknown: balanced Balance H: $Al \rightarrow Al^{3+}$ $\qquad\qquad 2H_3O^+ \rightarrow H_2 + 2H_2O$
$\qquad$ equation Balance e^-: $Al \rightarrow Al^{3+} + 3e^-$ $\qquad 2e^- + 2H_3O^+ \rightarrow H_2 + 2H_2O$

$$2[Al \rightarrow Al^{3+} + 3e^-]$$
$$\underline{3[2e^- + 2H_3O^+ \rightarrow H_2 + 2H_2O]}$$
$$2Al + 6H_3O^+ \rightarrow 3H_2 + 6H_2O$$

3. Given: $NaBr + H_2O_2 \rightarrow$ Sodium is a spectator ion and does not change its oxidation num-
$\qquad Br_2 + H_2O$ ber, so it is not included in the half-reactions.

Unknown: balanced
$\qquad$ equation Unbalanced: $2Br^- \rightarrow Br_2$ $\qquad\qquad H_2O_2 \rightarrow H_2O$
Balance O: $2Br^- \rightarrow Br_2$ $\qquad\qquad H_2O_2 \rightarrow 2H_2O$
Balance H: $2Br^- \rightarrow Br_2$ $\qquad\qquad 2H_3O^+ + H_2O_2 \rightarrow 4H_2O$
Balance e^-: $2Br^- \rightarrow Br_2 + 2e^-$ $\qquad 2e^- + 2H_3O^+ + H_2O_2 \rightarrow 4H_2O$

$$2Br^- \rightarrow Br_2 + 2e^-$$
$$\underline{2e^- + 2H_3O^+ + H_2O_2 \rightarrow 4H_2O}$$
$$2Br^- + 2H_3O^+ + H_2O_2 \rightarrow Br_2 + 4H_2O$$

4. Given: $MnO_2 + Cu^+ \rightarrow$ Unbalanced: $\qquad\qquad MnO_2 \rightarrow Mn^{2+}$ $\qquad Cu^+ \rightarrow Cu^{2+}$
$\qquad Mn^{2+} + Cu^{2+}$ Balance O: $\qquad\qquad MnO_2 \rightarrow Mn^{2+} + 2H_2O$ $\quad Cu^+ \rightarrow Cu^{2+}$

Unknown: balanced Balance H: $\qquad 4H_3O^+ + MnO_2 \rightarrow Mn^{2+} + 6H_2O$ $\quad Cu^+ \rightarrow Cu^{2+}$
$\qquad$ equation Balance e^-: $2e^- + 4H_3O^+ + MnO_2 \rightarrow Mn^{2+} + 6H_2O$ $\quad Cu^+ \rightarrow Cu^{2+} + e^-$

$$2e^- + 4H_3O^+ + MnO_2 \rightarrow Mn^{2+} + 6H_2O$$
$$\underline{2[Cu^+ \rightarrow Cu^{2+} + e^-]}$$
$$4H_3O^+ + MnO_2 + 2Cu^+ \rightarrow Mn^{2+} + 6H_2O + 2Cu^{2+}$$

Section 1 Review

6. a. Given: H_2SO_3 The oxidation number of the H atoms is +1. The oxidation num-

Unknown: oxidation ber of the O atoms is –2. The oxidation number of the S atom is
$\qquad$ number for unknown.
$\qquad$ each atom $\overset{+1 \ \ x-2}{H_2SO_3}$

Total oxidation number: $2(+1) + x + 3(-2) = 0$.

The oxidation number of the S atom is +4.

b. Given: Cl_2

Unknown: oxidation number for each atom

Cl_2 represents a free element in molecular form, so the **oxidation** number of the Cl atoms is 0.

c. Given: SF_6

Unknown: oxidation number for each atom

The oxidation number of the F atoms is -1. The **oxidation number** of the S atom is unknown.

$$\overset{x \; -1}{SF_6}$$

Total oxidation number: $x + 6(-1) = 0$.

The oxidation number of the S atom is $+6$.

d. Given: NO_3^-

Unknown: oxidation number for each atom

The oxidation number of the O atom is -2. The **oxidation number** of the N atom is unknown.

$$\overset{x \; -2}{NO_3^-}$$

Total oxidation number: $x + 3(-2) = -1$.

The oxidation number of the N atom is $+5$.

---

7. a. Given: CH_4

Unknown: oxidation number for each atom

The oxidation number of the H atoms is $+1$. The oxidation number of the C atom is unknown.

$$\overset{x \; +1}{CH_4}$$

Total oxidation number: $x + 4(+1) = 0$.

The oxidation number of the C atom is -4.

b. Given: HSO_3^-

Unknown: oxidation number for each atom

The oxidation number of the H atom is $+1$. The oxidation number of the O atoms is -2. The oxidation number of the S atom is unknown.

$$\overset{+1 \; x \; -2}{HSO_3^-}$$

Total oxidation number: $(+1) + x + 3(-2) = -1$.

The oxidation number of the S atom is $+4$.

c. Given: $NaHCO_3$

Unknown: oxidation number for each atom

The oxidation number of the Na atom is $+1$ because it is an atom of an element in Group 1. The oxidation number of the H atom is $+1$. The oxidation number of the O atoms is -2. The **oxidation** number of the C atom is unknown.

$$\overset{+1 \; +1 \; x \; -2}{NaHCO_3}$$

Total oxidation number: $(+1) + (+1) + x + 3(-2) = 0$.

The oxidation number of the C atom is $+4$.

d. Given: $NaBiO_3$

Unknown: oxidation number for each atom

The oxidation number of the Na atom is $+1$ because it is an atom of an element in Group 1. The oxidation number of the O atoms is -2. The oxidation number of the Bi atom is unknown.

$$\overset{+1 \; x \; -2}{NaBiO_3}$$

Total oxidation number: $(+1) + x + 3(-2) = 0$.

The oxidation number of the Bi atom is $+5$.

8. Given: substances composed of Cr

Unknown: the oxidation number of the Cr atom

$$\overset{x\ \ -2}{CrO_3}$$

Total oxidation number: $x + 3(-2) = 0$.

The oxidation number of the Cr atom is +6.

$$\overset{x\ \ -2}{CrO}$$

Total oxidation number: $x + (-2) = 0$.

The oxidation number of the Cr atom is +2.

Cr(s)

Cr(s) represents a free element in atomic form, so the oxidation number of the Cr atom is 0.

$$\overset{x\ \ -2}{CrO_2}$$

Total oxidation number: $x + 2(-2) = 0$.

The oxidation number of the Cr atom is +4.

$$\overset{x\ \ -2}{Cr_2O_3}$$

Total oxidation number: $2(x) + 3(-2) = 0$.

The oxidation number of the Cr atom is +3.

$$\overset{x\ \ -2}{Cr_2O_7^{2-}}$$

Total oxidation number: $2(x) + 7(-2) = -2$.

The oxidation number of the Cr atom is +6.

$$\overset{x\ \ -2}{Cr_2O_4^{2-}}$$

Total oxidation number: $x + 4(-2) = -2$.

The oxidation number of the Cr atom is +6.

9. Given: balanced equation

Unknown: if reaction is a redox reaction; if it is, then the atom oxidized, the atom reduced, the oxidizing agent, and the reducing agent

a. $MgO(s) + H_2CO_3(aq) \rightarrow MgCO_3(s) + H_2O(l)$

$$\overset{+2\ -2}{MgO} + \overset{+1\ +4-2}{H_2CO_3} \rightarrow \overset{+2\ +4-2}{MgCO_3} + \overset{+1\ -2}{H_2O}$$

not redox

b. $2KNO_3(s) \rightarrow 2KNO_2(s) + O_2(g)$

$$\overset{+1+5-2}{2KNO_3} \rightarrow \overset{+1+3-2}{2KNO_2} + \overset{0}{O_2}$$

redox; O is oxidized (-2 to 0), so NO_3^- is the reducing agent. N is reduced (+5 to +3), so NO_3^- is the oxidizing agent.

c. $H_2(g) + CuO(s) \rightarrow Cu(s) + H_2O(l)$

$$\overset{0}{H_2} + \overset{+2\ -2}{CuO} \rightarrow \overset{0}{Cu} + \overset{+1\ -2}{H_2O}$$

redox; H is oxidized (0 to +1), so H_2 is the reducing agent. Cu is reduced (+2 to 0), so Cu^{2+} is the oxidizing agent.

d. $NaOH(aq) + HCl(aq) \rightarrow NaCl(aq) + H_2O(l)$

$$\overset{+1\ -2+1}{NaOH} + \overset{+1-1}{HCl} \rightarrow \overset{+1\ -1}{NaCl} + \overset{+1\ -2}{H_2O}$$

not redox

e. $H_2(g) + Cl_2(g) \rightarrow 2HCl(g)$

$$\overset{0}{H_2} + \overset{0}{Cl_2} \rightarrow \overset{+1-1}{2HCl}$$

redox; H is oxidized (0 to +1), so H_2 is the reducing agent. Cl is reduced (0 to −1), so Cl_2 is the oxidizing agent.

f. $SO_3(g) + H_2O(l) \rightarrow H_2SO_4(aq)$

$$\overset{+6-2}{SO_3} + \overset{+1\ -2}{H_2O} \rightarrow \overset{+1\ +6-2}{H_2SO_4}$$

not redox

---

10. Given: unbalanced redox equation

Unknown: balanced equation

a. $Cl^-(aq) + Cr_2O_7^{2-}(aq) \rightarrow Cl_2(g) + Cr^{3+}(aq)$

Unbalanced: $2Cl^- \rightarrow Cl_2$		$Cr_2O_7^{2-} \rightarrow 2Cr^{3+}$
Balance O: $2Cl^- \rightarrow Cl_2$		$Cr_2O_7^{2-} \rightarrow 2Cr^{3+} + 7H_2O$
Balance H: $2Cl^- \rightarrow Cl_2$	$14H_3O^+ + Cr_2O_7^{2-} \rightarrow 2Cr^{3+} + 21H_2O$	
Balance e^-: $2Cl^- \rightarrow Cl_2 + 2e^-$		
	$6e^- + 14H_3O^+ + Cr_2O_7^{2-} \rightarrow 2Cr^{3+} + 21H_2O$	

$$3[2Cl^- \rightarrow Cl_2 + 2e^-]$$
$$\underline{6e^- + 14H_3O^+ + Cr_2O_7^{2-} \rightarrow 2Cr^{3+} + 21H_2O}$$
$$6Cl^- + 14H_3O^+ + Cr_2O_7^{2-} \rightarrow 3Cl_2 + 2Cr^{3+} + 21H_2O$$

b. $Cu(s) + Ag^+(aq) \rightarrow Cu^{2+}(aq) + Ag(s)$

Unbalanced: $Cu \rightarrow Cu^{2+}$	$Ag^+ \rightarrow Ag$
Balance O: $Cu \rightarrow Cu^{2+}$	$Ag^+ \rightarrow Ag$
Balance H: $Cu \rightarrow Cu^{2+}$	$Ag^+ \rightarrow Ag$
Balance e^-: $Cu \rightarrow Cu^{2+} + 2e^-$	$e^- + Ag^+ \rightarrow Ag$

$$Cu \rightarrow Cu^{2+} + 2e^-$$
$$\underline{2[e^- + Ag^+ \rightarrow Ag]}$$
$$Cu + 2Ag^+ \rightarrow Cu^{2+} + 2Ag$$

c. $Br_2(l) + I^-(aq) \rightarrow I_2(s) + Br^-(aq)$

Unbalanced:	$Br_2 \rightarrow 2Br^-$	$2I^- \rightarrow I_2$
Balance O:	$Br_2 \rightarrow 2Br^-$	$2I^- \rightarrow I_2$
Balance H:	$Br_2 \rightarrow 2Br^-$	$2I^- \rightarrow I_2$
Balance e^-:	$2e^- + Br_2 \rightarrow 2Br^-$	$2I^- \rightarrow I_2 + 2e^-$

$$2e^- + Br_2 \rightarrow 2Br^-$$
$$\underline{2I^- \rightarrow I_2 + 2e^-}$$
$$Br_2 + 2I^- \rightarrow 2Br^- + I_2$$

d. $I^-(aq) + NO_2^-(aq) \rightarrow NO(g) + I_2(s)$

Unbalanced: $2I^- \rightarrow I_2$	$NO_2^- \rightarrow NO$
Balance O: $2I^- \rightarrow I_2$	$NO_2^- \rightarrow NO + H_2O$
Balance H: $2I^- \rightarrow I_2$	$2H_3O^+ + NO_2^- \rightarrow NO + 3H_2O$
Balance e^-: $2I^- \rightarrow I_2 + 2e^-$	$e^- + 2H_3O^+ + NO_2^- \rightarrow NO + 3H_2O$

$$2I^- \rightarrow I_2 + 2e^-$$
$$\underline{2[e^- + 2H_3O^+ + NO_2^- \rightarrow NO + 3H_2O]}$$
$$2I^- + 4H_3O^+ + 2NO_2^- \rightarrow I_2 + 2NO + 6H_2O$$

Solutions Manual *continued*

Practice Problems C

1. Given: $Fe(s) \rightarrow Fe^{3+}(aq) + 3e^-$ and $O_2(g) + 2H_2O(l) + 4e^- \rightarrow 4OH^-(aq)$

Unknown: voltage of the cell

Electrode potentials:

$Fe^{3+}(aq) + 3e^- \rightleftharpoons Fe(s)$ $E° = -0.037$ V

$O_2(g) + 2H_2O(l) + 4e^- \rightleftharpoons 4OH^-(aq)$ $E° = +0.401$ V

The iron electrode is the anode as shown by the electrode reactions provided.

$E°_{cell} = E°_{O_2} - E°_{Fe} = (+0.401$ V$) - (-0.037$ V$) = +0.438$ V

---

2. Given: Cu in Cu^{2+} and Zn in Zn^{2+}

Unknown: voltage of the cell for the naturally occurring reaction

Electrode potentials:

$Cu^{2+}(aq) + 2e^- \rightleftharpoons Cu(s)$ $E° = +0.3419$ V

$Zn^{2+}(aq) + 2e^- \rightleftharpoons Zn(s)$ $E° = -0.7618$ V

The copper electrode has the more positive $E°$, so it is the cathode.

$E°_{cell} = E°_{Cu} - E°_{Zn} = (+0.3419$ V$) - (-0.7618$ V$) = +1.1037$ V

---

3. Given: Ag in Ag^+ and Cu in Cu^{2+}

Unknown: voltage of the cell for the naturally occurring reaction

Electrode potentials:

$Ag^{2+}(aq) + e^- \rightleftharpoons Ag(s)$ $E° = +0.7996$ V

$Cu^{2+}(aq) + 2e^- \rightleftharpoons Cu(s)$ $E° = +0.3419$ V

The silver electrode has the more positive $E°$, so it is the cathode.

$E°_{cell} = E°_{Ag} - E°_{Cu} = (+0.7996$ V$) - (+0.3419$ V$) = +0.4577$ V

Section 3 Review

5. Given: $Ag(s) + Cl^-(aq) \rightarrow AgCl(s) + e^-$ and $Cl_2(g) + 2e^- \rightarrow 2Cl^-(aq)$

Unknown: voltage of the cell

Electrode potentials:

$AgCl(s) + e^- \rightleftharpoons Ag(s) + Cl^-(aq)$ $E° = +0.222$ V

$Cl_2(g) + 2e^- \rightleftharpoons 2Cl^-(aq)$ $E° = +1.358$ V

The silver electrode is the anode as shown by the electrode reactions provided.

$E°_{cell} = E°_{Cl_2} - E°_{Ag} = (+1.358$ V$) - (+0.222$ V$) = +1.136$ V

---

6. Given: $Zn^{2+}(aq) + 2e^- \rightleftharpoons Zn(s)$ and $2H_2O(l) + 2e^- \rightleftharpoons H_2(g) + 2OH^-(aq)$

Unknown: voltage of the cell for the naturally occurring reactions

Electrode potentials:

$Zn^{2+}(aq) + 2e^- \rightleftharpoons Zn(s)$ $E° = -0.7618$ V

$2H_2O(l) + 2e^- \rightleftharpoons H_s(g) + 2OH^-(aq)$ $E° = -0.828$ V

The zinc electrode has the more positive $E°$, so it is the cathode.

$E°_{cell} = E°_{Zn} - E°_{H_2} = (-0.7618$ V$) - (-0.828$ V$) = +0.066$ V

| Solutions Manual *continued*

Chapter Review

39. Given: CO_2
Unknown: oxidation number for each atom

The oxidation number of the O atoms is –2. The oxidation number of the C atom is unknown.
$$\overset{x\ -2}{CO_2}$$
Total oxidation number: $x + 2(-2) = 0$.

The oxidation number of the C atom is +4.

40. Given: CoO
Unknown: oxidation number for each atom

The oxidation number of the O atoms is –2. The oxidation number of the Co atom is unknown.
$$\overset{x\ -2}{CoO}$$
Total oxidation number: $x + (-2) = 0$.

The oxidation number of the Co atom is +2.

41. Given: $BaCl_2$
Unknown: oxidation number for each atom

The oxidation number of the Ba atom is +2 because it is an atom of an element in Group 2. The oxidation number of the Cl atoms is –1.

Total oxidation number: $(+2) + 2(-1) = 0$.

42. Given: K_2SO_4
Unknown: oxidation number for each atom

The oxidation number of the K atoms is +1 because they are atoms of an element in Group 1. The oxidation number of the O atoms is –2. The oxidation number of the S atom is unknown.
$$\overset{+1\ \ x-2}{K_2SO_4}$$
Total oxidation number: $2(+1) + x + 4(-2) = 0$.

The oxidation number of the S atom is +6.

43. Given: S^{2-}
Unknown: oxidation number for each atom

S^{2-} is a monatomic ion, so the oxidation number is equal to the charge. The oxidation number of the S atom is –2.

44. Given: La^{3+}
Unknown: oxidation number for each atom

La^{3+} is a monatomic ion, so the oxidation number is equal to the charge. The oxidation number of the La atom is +3.

45. Given: CH_4
Unknown: oxidation number for each atom

The oxidation number of the H atoms is +1. The oxidation number of the C atom is unknown.
$$\overset{x\ +1}{CH_4}$$
Total oxidation number: $x + 4(+1) = 0$.

The oxidation number of the C atom is –4.

Solutions Manual *continued*

46. Given: NH_4^+

Unknown: oxidation number for each atom

The oxidation number of the H atoms is +1. The oxidation number of the N atom is unknown.

$$\overset{x}{N}\overset{+1}{H_4^+}$$

Total oxidation number: $x + 4(+1) = +1$.

The oxidation number of the N atom is –3.

---

47. Given: $CaCO_3$

Unknown: oxidation number for each atom

The oxidation number of the Ca atom is +2 because it is an atom of an element in Group 2. The oxidation number of the O atoms is –2. The oxidation number of the C atom is unknown.

$$\overset{+2}{Ca}\overset{x}{C}\overset{-2}{O_3}$$

Total oxidation number: $(+2) + x + 3(-2) = 0$.

The oxidation number of the C atom is +4.

---

48. Given: $PtCl_6^{2-}$

Unknown: oxidation number for each atom

The oxidation number of the Cl atoms is –1. The oxidation number of the Pt atom is unknown.

$$\overset{x}{Pt}\overset{-1}{Cl_6^{2-}}$$

Total oxidation number: $x + 6(-1) = -2$.

The oxidation number of the Pt atom is +4.

---

49. Given: $COCl_2$

Unknown: oxidation number for each atom

The oxidation number of the O atom is –2. The oxidation number of the Cl atoms is –1. The oxidation number of the C atom is unknown.

$$\overset{x}{C}\overset{-2}{O}\overset{-1}{Cl_2}$$

Total oxidation number: $x + (-2) + 2(-1) = 0$.

The oxidation number of the C atom is +4.

---

50. Given: PO_4^{3-}

Unknown: oxidation number for each atom

The oxidation number of the O atoms is –2. The oxidation number of the P atom is unknown.

$$\overset{x}{P}\overset{-2}{O_4^{3-}}$$

Total oxidation number: $x + 4(-2) = -3$.

The oxidation number of the P atom is +5.

---

51. Given: Fe(s) changes to $Fe^{2+}(aq)$

Unknown: balanced half-reaction

Unbalanced: $Fe \rightarrow Fe^{2+}$
Balance O: $Fe \rightarrow Fe^{2+}$
Balance H: $Fe \rightarrow Fe^{2+}$
Balance e^-: $Fe \rightarrow Fe^{2+} + 2e^-$

---

52. Given: $Cl_2(g)$ changes to $Cl^-(aq)$

Unknown: balanced half-reaction

Unbalanced: $Cl_2 \rightarrow 2Cl^-$
Balance O: $Cl_2 \rightarrow 2Cl^-$
Balance H: $Cl_2 \rightarrow 2Cl^-$
Balance e^-: $Cl_2 + 2e^- \rightarrow 2Cl^-$

Solutions Manual *continued*

53. Given: $Fe \rightarrow Fe^{2+} + 2e^-$
and $Cl_2 + 2e^- \rightarrow 2Cl^-$
Unknown: overall
equation

$Fe \rightarrow Fe^{2+} + 2e^-$
$\underline{Cl_2 + 2e^- \rightarrow 2Cl^-}$
$Fe + Cl_2 \rightarrow Fe^{2+} + 2Cl^-$

---

54. Given: $HOBr(aq)$ changes
to $Br_2(aq)$
Unknown: balanced half-
reaction

Unbalanced: $\qquad\qquad 2HOBr \rightarrow Br_2$
Balance O: $\qquad\qquad 2HOBr \rightarrow Br_2 + 2H_2O$
Balance H: $\qquad 2H_3O^+ + 2HOBr \rightarrow Br_2 + 4H_2O$
Balance e^-: $2e^- + 2H_3O^+ + 2HOBr \rightarrow Br_2 + 4H_2O$

---

55. Given: $H_2O(l)$ changes to
$O_2(aq)$
Unknown: balanced half-
reaction

Unbalanced: $\ H_2O \rightarrow O_2$
Balance O: $\ 2H_2O \rightarrow O_2$
Balance H: $\ 6H_2O \rightarrow O_2 + 4H_3O^+$
Balance e^-: $\ 6H_2O \rightarrow O_2 + 4H_3O^+ + 4e^-$

---

56. Given: $2e^- + 2H_3O +$
$2HOBr \rightarrow Br_2 + 4H_2O$
and $6H_2O \rightarrow O_2 +$
$4H_3O^+ + 4e^-$
Unknown: overall
equation

$2[2e^- + 2H_3O^+ + 2HOBr \rightarrow Br_2 + 4H_2O]$
$\underline{\qquad\qquad 6H_2O \rightarrow O_2 + 4H_3O^+ + 4e^-}$
$\qquad 4HOBr \rightarrow 2Br_2 + 2H_2O + O_2$

---

57. Given: $O_2(aq)$ changes to
$H_2O(l)$
Unknown: balanced half-
reaction

Unbalanced: $\qquad\qquad O_2 \rightarrow H_2O$
Balance O: $\qquad\qquad O_2 \rightarrow 2H_2O$
Balance H: $\qquad 4H_3O^+ + O_2 \rightarrow 6H_2O$
Balance e^-: $4e^- + 4H_3O^+ + O_2 \rightarrow 6H_2O$

---

58. Given: $SO_2(aq)$ changes
to $HSO_4^-(aq)$
Unknown: balanced half-
reaction

Unbalanced: $\qquad\qquad SO_2 \rightarrow HSO_4^-$
Balance O: $\ 2H_2O + SO_2 \rightarrow HSO_4^-$
Balance H: $\ 5H_2O + SO_2 \rightarrow HSO_4^- + 3H_3O^+$
Balance e^-: $\ 5H_2O + SO_2 \rightarrow HSO_4^- + 3H_3O^+ + 2e^-$

---

59. Given: $4e^- + 4H_3O^+ +$
$O_2 \rightarrow 6H_2O$
and $5H_2O + SO_2 \rightarrow$
$HSO_4^- + 3H_3O^+ + 2e^-$
Unknown: overall
equation

$4e^- + 4H_3O^+ + O_2 \rightarrow 6H_2O$
$\underline{2[5H_2O + SO_2 \rightarrow HSO_4^- + 3H_3O^+ + 2e^-]}$
$O_2 + 4H_2O + 2SO_2 \rightarrow 2HSO_4^- + 2H_3O^+$

---

60. Given: $Zn(s) + Fe^{3+}(aq) \rightarrow$
$Zn^{2+}(aq) + Fe^{2+}(aq)$
Unknown: balanced
equation

Unbalanced: $Zn \rightarrow Zn^{2+}$ $\qquad\qquad Fe^{3+} \rightarrow Fe^{2+}$
Balance O: $\ Zn \rightarrow Zn^{2+}$ $\qquad\qquad Fe^{3+} \rightarrow Fe^{2+}$
Balance H: $\ Zn \rightarrow Zn^{2+}$ $\qquad\qquad Fe^{3+} \rightarrow Fe^{2+}$
Balance e^-: $\ Zn \rightarrow Zn^{2+} + 2e^-$ $\quad e^- + Fe^{3+} \rightarrow Fe^{2+}$

$Zn \rightarrow Zn^{2+} + 2e^-$
$\underline{2[e^- + Fe^{3+} \rightarrow Fe^{2+}]}$
$Zn + 2Fe^{3+} \rightarrow Zn^{2+} + 2Fe^{2+}$

---

61. Given: standard electrode
potentials 1.30 V
and 0.45 V
Unknown: voltage of
the cell

The electrode that has the more positive $E°$ (1.30 V) is the
cathode.

$E°_{cell} = E°_{cathode} - E°_{anode} = (1.30\ V) - (0.45\ V) = 0.85\ V$

Solutions Manual *continued*

62. Given: $AgCl(s) + e^- \rightleftharpoons$
$Ag(s) + Cl^-(aq)$
and $2H_3O^+(aq) + 2e^- \rightleftharpoons$
$2H_2O(l) + H_2(g)$

Unknown: voltage of
the cell for
the naturally
occurring
reaction

Electrode potentials:

$AgCl(s) + e^- \rightleftharpoons Ag(s) + Cl^-(aq)$ $E^\circ = +0.222V$

$2H_3O^+(aq) + 2e^- \rightleftharpoons 2H_2O(l) + H_2(g)$ $E^\circ = 0.0000$ V

The silver electrode has the more positive E°, so it is the cathode.

$E^\circ_{cell} = E^\circ_{Ag} - E^\circ_{H_2} = (+0.222$ V$) - (0.0000$ V$) = +0.222$ V

63. Given: $2H_3O^+(aq) + 2e^- \rightarrow$
$2H_2O(l) + H_2(g)$
and $Fe^{2+}(aq) \rightarrow Fe^{3+}(aq) + e^-$

Unknown: voltage of the
cell

Electrode potentials:

$2H_3O^+(aq) + 2e^- \rightleftharpoons 2H_2O(l) + H_2(g)$ $E^\circ = 0.0000$ V

$Fe^{3+}(aq) + e^- \rightleftharpoons Fe^{2+}(aq)$ $E^\circ = +0.771$ V

The iron electrode is the anode as shown by the electrode reactions provided.

$E^\circ_{cell} = E^\circ_{H_2} - E^\circ_{Fe} = (+0.0000$ V$) - (+0.771$ V$) = -0.771$ V

64. Given: $2Fe^{3+}(aq) + Cd(s)$
$\rightarrow Cd^{2+}(aq) + 2Fe^{2+}(aq)$

Unknown: voltage of the
cell

Electrode potentials:

$Fe^{3+}(aq) + e^- \rightleftharpoons Fe^{2+}(aq)$ $E^\circ = +0.771$ V

$Cd^{2+}(aq) + 2e^- \rightleftharpoons Cd(s)$ $E^\circ = -0.4030$ V

The iron electrode is the cathode as shown by the equation provided.

$E^\circ_{cell} = E^\circ_{Fe} - E^\circ_{Cd} = (+0.771$ V$) - (-0.4030$ V$) = +1.174$ V

65. Given: $O_2(g) + 2H_2O(l) +$
$4e^- \rightarrow 4OH^-(aq)$
and $H_2(g) + 2OH^-(aq) \rightarrow$
$2H_2O(l) + 2e^-$

Unknown: voltage of the
cell

Electrode potentials:

$O_2(g) + 2H_2O(l) + 4e^- \rightleftharpoons 4OH^-(aq)$ $E^\circ = +0.401$ V

$2H_2O(l) + 2e^- \rightleftharpoons H_2(g) + 2OH^-(aq)$ $E^\circ = -0.828$ V

The oxygen electrode is the cathode as shown by the electrode reactions provided.

$E^\circ_{cell} = E^\circ_{O_2} - E^\circ_{H_2} = (+0.401$ V$) - (-0.828$ V$) = +1.229$ V

66. Given: chlorine is
reduced to
chloride ions, and
copper is oxidized
to copper(II) ions

Unknown: voltage of the
cell

Electrode potentials:

$Cl_2(g) + 2e^- \rightleftharpoons 2Cl^-(aq)$ $E^\circ = +1.358$ V

$Cu^{2+}(aq) + 2e^- \rightleftharpoons Cu(s)$ $E^\circ = +0.3419$ V

The copper electrode is the anode because copper is oxidized.

$E^\circ_{cell} = E^\circ_{Cl_2} - E^\circ_{Cu} = (+1.358$ V$) - (+0.3419$ V$) = +1.016$ V

Solutions Manual *continued*

67. Given: the electrode reactions of a lead-acid battery

Unknown: voltage of the cell

Electrode reactions:

$$PbO_2(s) + HSO_4^-(aq) + 3H_3O^+(aq) + 2e^- \rightarrow PbSO_4(s) + 5H_2O(l)$$

$$Pb(s) + HSO_4^-(aq) + H_2O(l) \rightarrow 2e^- + PbSO_4(s) + H_3O^+(aq)$$

Electrode potentials:

$$PbO_2(s) + HSO_4^-(aq) + 3H_3O^+(aq) + 2e^- \rightleftharpoons PbSO_4(s) + 5H_2O(l)$$
$$E° = +1.691 \text{ V}$$

$$PbSO_4(s) + H_3O^+(aq) + 2e^- \rightleftharpoons Pb(s) + HSO_4^-(aq) + H_2O(l)$$
$$E° = -0.42 \text{ V}$$

The PbO_2 electrode is where reduction occurs, so it is the cathode.

$$E°_{cell} = E°_{PbO_2} - E°_{Pb} = (+1.691 \text{ V}) - (-0.42 \text{ V}) = +2.11 \text{ V}$$

68. Given: oxides of nitrogen

Unknown: the oxidation number of the N atom

$\overset{x}{N_2}\overset{-2}{O}$

Total oxidation number: $2(x) + (-2) = 0$.

The oxidation number of the N atoms is +1.

$\overset{x}{N}\overset{-2}{O}$

Total oxidation number: $x + (-2) = 0$.

The oxidation number of the N atom is +2.

$\overset{x}{N}\overset{-2}{O_2}$

Total oxidation number: $x + (-2) = 0$.

The oxidation number of the N atom is +4.

$\overset{x}{N_2}\overset{-2}{O_3}$

Total oxidation number: $2(x) + 3(-2) = 0$.

The oxidation number of the N atoms is +3.

$\overset{x}{N_2}\overset{-2}{O_4}$

Total oxidation number: $2(x) + 4(-2) = 0$.

The oxidation number of the N atom is +4.

$\overset{x}{N_2}\overset{-2}{O_5}$

Total oxidation number: $2(x) + 5(-2) = 0$.

The oxidation number of the N atoms is +5.

75. a. Given: P_4

Unknown: oxidation number for each atom

P_4 represents a free element in molecular form, so the oxidation number of the P atoms is 0.

b. Given: H_2SO_3

Unknown: oxidation number for each atom

The oxidation number of the H atoms is +1. The oxidation number of the O atoms is –2. The oxidation number of the S atom is unknown.

$$\overset{+1\ \ x\ -2}{H_2SO_3}$$

Total oxidation number: $2(+1) + x + 3(-2) = 0$.

The oxidation number of the S atom is +4.

---

78. Given: $Cr_2O_7^{2-}(aq) + Fe^{2+}(aq) \rightarrow Cr^{3+}(aq) + Fe^{3+}(aq)$

Unknown: balanced equation

Unbalanced: $Fe^{2+} \rightarrow Fe^{3+}$ $\qquad Cr_2O_7^{2-} \rightarrow 2Cr^{3+}$

Balance O: $Fe^{2+} \rightarrow Fe^{3+}$ $\qquad Cr_2O_7^{2-} \rightarrow 2Cr^{3+} + 7H_2O$

Balance H: $Fe^{2+} \rightarrow Fe^{3+}$

$$14H_3O^+ + Cr_2O_7^{2-} \rightarrow 2Cr^{3+} + 21H_2O$$

Balance e^-: $Fe^{2+} \rightarrow Fe^{3+} + e^-$

$$6e^- + 14H_3O^+ + Cr_2O_7^{2-} \rightarrow 2Cr^{3+} + 21H_2O$$

$$6[Fe^{2+} \rightarrow Fe^{3+} + e^-]$$

$$\underline{6e^- + 14H_3O^+ + Cr_2O_7^{2-} \rightarrow 2Cr^{3+} + 21H_2O}$$

$$6Fe^{2+} + 14H_3O^+ + Cr_2O_7^{2-} \rightarrow 6Fe^{3+} + 2Cr^{3+} + 21H_2O$$

---

79. Given: $CdCl_2(aq) \rightarrow Cd(s) + Cl_2(g)$

Unknown: voltage of the cell

Electrode potentials:

$$Cd^{2+}(aq) + 2e^- \rightleftharpoons Cd(s) \qquad\qquad E° = -0.4030 \text{ V}$$

$$Cl_2(g) + 2e^- \rightleftharpoons 2Cl^-(aq) \qquad\qquad E° = +1.358 \text{ V}$$

The cadmium electrode is the cathode because $Cd(s)$ is formed in the overall reaction for the electrolysis of $CdCl_2$.

$$E°_{cell} = E°_{Cd} - E°_{Cl_2} = (-0.4030 \text{ V}) - (+1.358 \text{ V}) = -1.761 \text{ V}$$

---

80. Given: $2AgCl(s) \rightarrow 2Ag(s) + Cl_2(g)$

Unknown: voltage of the cell

Electrode potentials:

$$AgCl(s) + e^- \rightleftharpoons Ag(s) + Cl^-(aq) \qquad E° = +0.222 \text{ V}$$

$$Cl_2(g) + 2e^- \rightleftharpoons 2Cl^-(aq) \qquad\qquad E° = +1.358 \text{ V}$$

The silver electrode is the cathode because $AgCl(s)$ is the reactant and $Ag(s)$ is formed in the overall reaction for the electrolysis of $AgCl$.

$$E°_{cell} = E°_{Ag} - E°_{Cl_2} = (+0.222 \text{ V}) - (+1.358 \text{ V}) = -1.136 \text{ V}$$

Problem Bank

1. Given: formula of HNO_2

Unknown: oxidation numbers for each atom

O has an oxidation number of –2. H has an oxidation number of +1.

$$\overset{+1\ \ -2}{HNO_2}$$

total oxidation number of oxygen atoms = $-2 \times 2 = -4$

total oxidation number of hydrogen atoms = $+1$

$$\underset{+1+3-4}{\overset{+1\ \ \ -2}{HNO_2}} \rightarrow \underset{+1+3-4}{\overset{+1+3-2}{HNO_2}}$$

N therefore has an oxidation number of +3.

---

2. Given: formula of H_2SO_3

Unknown: oxidation numbers

O has an oxidation number of –2. H has an oxidation number of +1.

$\overset{+1-2}{H_2SO_3}$

total oxidation number of oxygen atoms = $-2 \times 3 = -6$

total oxidation number of hydrogen atoms = $+1 \times 2 = +2$

$\underset{+2\ +4\,-6}{\overset{+1-2}{H_2SO_3}} \rightarrow \underset{+2\ +4\,-6}{\overset{+1\ +4-2}{H_2SO_3}}$

S therefore has an oxidation number of +4.

3. Given: formula of H_2CO_3

Unknown: oxidation numbers

O has an oxidation number of –2. H has an oxidation number of +1.

$\overset{+1-2}{H_2CO_3}$

total oxidation number of oxygen atoms = $-2 \times 3 = -6$

total oxidation number of hydrogen atoms = $+1 \times 2 = +2$

$\underset{+2\ +4\,-6}{\overset{+1-2}{H_2CO_3}} \rightarrow \underset{+2\ +4\,-6}{\overset{+1\ +4-2}{H_2CO_3}}$

C therefore has an oxidation number of +4.

4. Given: formula of HI

Unknown: oxidation numbers

I can be treated as an anion with an oxidation number of –1. H has an oxidation number of +1.

H, +1

I, –1

5. Given: formula of CO_2

Unknown: oxidation numbers

O has an oxidation number of –2.

$\overset{-2}{CO_2}$

total oxidation number of oxygen atoms = $-2 \times 2 = -4$

$\underset{+4-4}{\overset{-2}{CO_2}} \rightarrow \underset{+4-4}{\overset{+4-2}{CO_2}}$

C therefore has an oxidation number of +4.

C, +4

O, –2

6. Given: formula of NH_4^+

Unknown: oxidation numbers

H has an oxidation number of +1.

$$\overset{+1}{N}H_4^+$$

total oxidation number of hydrogen atoms

$= +1 \times 4 = +4$

$$\overset{+1}{\underset{+4}{N}}H_4^+$$

balance of oxidation numbers

$$\overset{+1}{\underset{-3+4}{N}}H_4^+ \rightarrow \overset{-3+1}{\underset{-3+4}{N}}H_4^+$$

N therefore has an oxidation number of –3.

N, –3

H, +1

---

7. Given: formula of MnO_4^-

Unknown: oxidation numbers

O has an oxidation number of –2.

$$Mn\overset{-2}{O}_4^-$$

total oxidation number of oxygen atoms $= -2 \times 4 = -8$

$$Mn\overset{-2}{\underset{-8}{O}}_4^-$$

balance of oxidation numbers

$$Mn\overset{-2}{\underset{+7\ -8}{O}}_4^- \rightarrow \overset{+7}{Mn}\overset{-2}{\underset{+7\ -8}{O}}_4^-$$

Mn therefore has an oxidation number of +7.

Mn, +7

O, –2

---

8. Given: formula of $S_2O_3^{2-}$

Unknown: oxidation numbers

O has an oxidation number of –2.

$$S_2\overset{-2}{O}_3^{2-}$$

total oxidation number of oxygen atoms $= -2 \times 3 = -6$

$$S_2\overset{-2}{\underset{-6}{O}}_3^{2-}$$

balance of oxidation numbers

$$S_2\overset{-2}{\underset{+4\ -6}{O}}_3^{2-} \rightarrow \overset{+2}{S_2}\overset{-2}{\underset{+4\ -6}{O}}_3^{2-}$$

S therefore has an oxidation number of +2.

S, +2

O, –2

9. Given: formula of H_2O_2

Unknown: oxidation numbers

O in peroxides has an oxidation number of –1.

$$\overset{-1}{H_2O_2}$$

total oxidation number of oxygen atoms = $-1 \times 2 = -2$

$$\overset{-1}{H_2\underset{-2}{O}_2}$$

balance of oxidation numbers

$$\underset{+2\ -2}{\overset{-1}{H_2O_2}} \rightarrow \underset{+2\ -2}{\overset{+1\ -1}{H_2O_2}}$$

H therefore has an oxidation number of +1.

H, +1

O, –1

10. Given: formula of P_4O_{10}

Unknown: oxidation numbers

O has an oxidation number of –2.

$$\overset{-2}{P_4O_{10}}$$

total oxidation number of oxygen atoms = $-2 \times 10 = -20$

$$\overset{-2}{P_4\underset{-20}{O}_{10}}$$

balance of oxidation numbers

$$\underset{+20\,-20}{\overset{-2}{P_4O_{10}}} \rightarrow \underset{+20\,-20}{\overset{+5\,-2}{P_4O_{10}}}$$

P therefore has an oxidation number of +5.

P, +5

O, –2

11. Given: formula of OF_2

Unknown: oxidation numbers

F always has an oxidation number of –1.

$$\overset{-1}{OF_2}$$

total oxidation number of fluorine atoms = $-1 \times 2 = -2$

$$\overset{-1}{O\underset{-2}{F}_2}$$

balance of oxidation numbers

$$\underset{+2\,-2}{\overset{-1}{OF_2}} \rightarrow \underset{+2\,-2}{\overset{+2\,-1}{OF_2}}$$

O therefore has an oxidation number of +2.

O, +2

F, –1

12. Given: formula of SO_3

Unknown: oxidation numbers

O has an oxidation number of -2.

$$\overset{-2}{S}O_2$$

total oxidation number of oxygen atoms $= -2 \times 3 = -6$

$$\underset{-6}{\overset{-2}{S}O_2} \rightarrow \underset{+6-6}{\overset{+6-2}{S}O_2}$$

S therefore has an oxidation number of $+6$.

---

13. Given: cadmium sulfide CdS

Unknown: oxidation state of cadmium

The sulfide has a charge of -2, so the oxidation number for Cd is $+2$.

---

14. Given: zinc sulfide ZnS

Unknown: oxidation state of zinc

The sulfide has a charge of -2, so the oxidation number for Zn is $+2$.

---

15. Given: lead chromate, $PbCrO_4$

Unknown: oxidation states of lead and chromium

The chromate ion has a charge of -2, so the oxidation number for Pb is $+2$.

For CrO_4^{2-}:

O in the CrO_4^{2+} ion has an oxidation number of -2, and the total oxidation number for the four oxygen atoms is -8. Balancing the oxidation numbers yields the following

$$\underset{-8}{\overset{-2}{Cr}O_4^{2-}} \rightarrow \underset{+6\,-8}{\overset{+6\,-2}{Cr}O_4^{2-}}$$

$Pb = +2$

$Cr = +6$

---

16. Given: $Fe(SCN)^{2+}$

Unknown: oxidation state of iron

For $Fe(SCN)^{2+}$, SCN can be assumed to have an oxidation number equal to its ionic charge of -1. Therefore, Fe must have an oxidation number of $+3$.

---

17. Given: MnO_4^-

Unknown: oxidation state of Mn

For MnO_4^-, O has an oxidation number of -2. Therefore, Mn must have an oxidation number of $+7$.

---

18. Given: $CoCl_2$

Unknown: oxidation state of Co

For $CoCl_2$, Cl has an oxidation number equal to its ionic charge of -1, Cu must have an oxidation number of $+2$.

---

19. Given: $[Cu(NH_3)_4](OH)_2$

Unknown: oxidation state of copper

Because NH_3 has no net charge, and OH has an oxidation number equal to its ionic charge of -1, Cu must have an oxidation number of $+2$.

---

20. Given: N_2O_3

Unknown: oxidation state of nitrogen

O has an oxidation number of -2. For N_2O_3, the total oxidation number for the O atoms is -6. Therefore, nitrogen has an oxidation state of $+3$.

$$\underset{-6}{\overset{-2}{N_2}O_3} \rightarrow \underset{+6\,-6}{\overset{+3\,-2}{N_2}O_3}$$

21. Given: N_2O_5

    Unknown: oxidation state
of nitrogen

O has an oxidation number of –2. For N_2O_5, the total oxidation number for the O atoms is –10. Therefore, nitrogen has an oxidation state of +5.

$$\overset{-2}{\underset{-10}{N_2}}\overset{}{O_5} \rightarrow \overset{+5\ -2}{\underset{+10\ -10}{N_2O_5}}$$

22.

a. $2KNO_3(s) \longrightarrow 2KNO_2(s) + O_2(g)$

$$\overset{+1+5-2}{2KNO_3} \longrightarrow \overset{+1+3-2}{2KNO_2} + \overset{0}{O_2}$$

$$\overset{-2}{2O} \longrightarrow \overset{0}{O_2} + 4e^-$$

$$\overset{+5}{2N} + 4e^- \longrightarrow \overset{+3}{2N}$$

redox

b. $H_2(g) + CuO(s) \longrightarrow Cu(s) + H_2O(l)$

$$\overset{0}{H_2(g)} + \overset{+2\ -2}{CuO(s)} \longrightarrow \overset{0}{Cu(s)} + \overset{+1\ -2}{H_2O(l)}$$

$$\overset{0}{H_2} \longrightarrow \overset{+1}{2H} + 2e^-$$

$$\overset{+2}{Cu} + 2e^- \longrightarrow \overset{0}{Cu}$$

redox

c. $NaOH(aq) + HCl(aq) \longrightarrow NaCl(aq) + H_2O(l)$

$$\overset{+1\ -2+1}{NaOH} + \overset{+1-1}{HCl} \longrightarrow \overset{+1\ -1}{NaCl} + \overset{+1\ -2}{H_2O}$$

not redox

d. $H_2(g) + Cl_2(g) \longrightarrow 2HCl(g)$

$$\overset{0}{H_2} + \overset{0}{Cl_2} \longrightarrow \overset{+1-1}{2HCl}$$

$$\overset{0}{H_2} \longrightarrow \overset{+1}{2H} + 2e^-$$

$$\overset{0}{Cl_2} + 2e^- \longrightarrow \overset{-1}{2Cl}$$

redox

e. $SO_3(g) + H_2O(l) \longrightarrow H_2SO_4(aq)$

$$\overset{+6-2}{SO_3} + \overset{+1\ -2}{H_2O} \longrightarrow \overset{+1\ +6-2}{H_2SO_4}$$

not redox

23.

a. $2NH_4Cl(aq) + Ca(OH)_2(aq) \longrightarrow 2NH_3(aq) + 2H_2O(l) + CaCl_2(aq)$

Ionic equation:

$$\overset{-3+1}{2NH_4^+} + \overset{-1}{Cl^-} + \overset{+2}{Ca^{+2}} + \overset{-2+1}{2OH^-} \longrightarrow \overset{-3+1}{2NH_3} + \overset{+1\ -2}{2H_2O} + \overset{+2}{Ca^{2+}} + \overset{-1}{2Cl^-}$$

nonredox

b. $2HNO_3(aq) + 3H_2S(g) \longrightarrow 2NO(g) + 4H_2O(l) + 3S(s)$

Ionic equation:

$$\overset{+1}{2H^+} + \overset{+5-2}{NO_3^-} + \overset{+2\ -2}{3H_2S} \longrightarrow \overset{+2-2}{2NO} + \overset{+1\ -2}{4H_2O} + \overset{0}{3S}$$

$$\overset{+5}{2NO_3^-} + 6e^- \longrightarrow \overset{+2}{2NO}$$

$$\overset{-2}{3H_2S} \longrightarrow \overset{0}{3S} + 6e^-$$

redox

c. $[Be(H_2O)_4]^{2+}(aq) + H_2O(l) \longrightarrow H_3O^+(aq) + [Be(H_2O)_3OH]^+(aq)$

Ionic equation:

$$\overset{+2\ +1\ -2}{[Be(H_2O)_4]^{2+}} + \overset{+1\ -2}{H_2O} \longrightarrow \overset{+1\ -2}{H_3O^+} + \overset{+2\ +1\ -2\ -2+1}{[Be(H_2O)_3OH]^+}$$

nonredox